THE CYBERSECURITY ANALYST'S HANDBOOK

Defend Against Cyber Threats with Pen Testing and Risk Management

THOMPSON CARTER

TABLE OF CONTENTS

INTRODUCTION

WELCOME TO THE FRONT LINES: YOUR JOURNEY INTO THE CYBERSECURITY BATTLEFIELD

The digital world is a battlefield. Every day, unseen forces wage war, attempting to breach defenses, steal valuable data, and disrupt the systems that underpin our modern lives. This is the reality of cybersecurity – a dynamic, ever-evolving field where the stakes are high, and the need for skilled defenders is critical.

This book is your field manual for navigating this complex landscape. Whether you're an aspiring cybersecurity analyst, a seasoned professional, or simply a curious individual seeking to understand the digital threats we face, this handbook will equip you with the knowledge, skills, and insights to become a formidable force in the fight for a safer digital world.

Why Cybersecurity Matters

In today's interconnected world, cybersecurity is no longer just an IT issue; it's a societal issue that affects everyone. From individuals and businesses to governments and critical infrastructure, we all rely on technology for our daily lives, making us all vulnerable to cyber threats.

Consider the following scenarios:

- A hacker gains access to your bank account, draining your savings and leaving you financially devastated.
- A ransomware attack cripples a hospital's systems, delaying critical care and putting patients' lives at risk.
- A nation-state launches a cyberattack on a country's power grid, causing widespread blackouts and disrupting essential services.
- A data breach exposes the personal information of millions of individuals, leading to identity theft and financial fraud.

These are not hypothetical scenarios; they are real-world examples of the devastating consequences of cyberattacks. The cost of cybercrime is estimated to reach trillions of dollars annually, and the impact on individuals, organizations, and societies can be profound.

The Evolving Threat Landscape

The cybersecurity landscape is constantly evolving, with new threats emerging and existing threats becoming more sophisticated. Attackers are becoming more organized, resourceful, and motivated, employing advanced techniques to bypass traditional security measures.

- **Malware:** Malicious software continues to evolve, from viruses and worms to ransomware and spyware, designed to steal data, disrupt systems, or extort money.

- **Phishing and Social Engineering:** Attackers are becoming increasingly adept at social engineering and phishing attacks, tricking users into revealing sensitive information or downloading malware.

- **Denial-of-Service Attacks:** DDoS attacks are becoming more frequent and powerful, overwhelming systems and disrupting critical services.

- **Advanced Persistent Threats (APTs):** Well-resourced attackers, often nation-state sponsored, are launching APTs to gain long-term access to sensitive systems and steal valuable data.

- **Exploiting Emerging Technologies:** Attackers are exploiting vulnerabilities in emerging technologies, such as cloud computing, IoT, and AI, to launch new and sophisticated attacks.

The Cybersecurity Imperative

The need for skilled cybersecurity professionals has never been greater. Organizations across all sectors are seeking individuals with the expertise to protect their systems, data, and reputations from cyber threats.

This book is your guide to entering and thriving in this exciting and challenging field. It provides a comprehensive overview of cybersecurity, covering:

- **Foundational Concepts:** We'll explore the fundamental principles of cybersecurity, including confidentiality, integrity, and availability, and delve into the evolving threat landscape.

- **Essential Skills:** You'll learn about the technical skills needed to defend against cyberattacks, including network security, operating system security, cryptography, and security tools.

- **Advanced Concepts:** We'll delve into advanced cybersecurity topics, such as cloud security, data security and privacy, application security, and incident response.

- **Emerging Trends:** We'll examine the cybersecurity implications of emerging technologies, including AI, IoT, blockchain, and quantum computing.

- **Career Development:** We'll guide you through the steps to building a successful cybersecurity career, from education and certifications to skills development and job roles.

- **Ethics and Professionalism:** We'll emphasize the importance of ethical conduct, responsible disclosure, and adherence to professional codes of conduct.

- **Continuous Learning:** We'll stress the necessity of staying up-to-date with the latest threats and technologies, participating in cybersecurity communities, and actively pursuing professional development.

Your Role in the Cybersecurity Ecosystem

Cybersecurity is a shared responsibility. Everyone has a role to play in creating a safer digital world, from individuals practicing good cyber hygiene to organizations implementing strong security controls and governments developing cybersecurity policies and regulations.

This book empowers you to become an active participant in the cybersecurity ecosystem. Whether you choose to pursue a career in cybersecurity or simply want to be a more informed and responsible digital citizen, the knowledge and skills you gain from this handbook will enable you to contribute to a more secure and resilient digital future.

Embark on Your Cybersecurity Journey

This book is your passport to the exciting and challenging world of cybersecurity. It's a field that demands continuous learning, adaptability, and a passion for protecting our digital world. As you embark on this journey, remember that cybersecurity is not just about technology; it's about people, ethics, and the collective effort to safeguard our interconnected world.

Welcome to the front lines. The battle for a safer digital future awaits.

CHAPTER 1: INTRODUCTION TO CYBERSECURITY

WHAT IS CYBERSECURITY?

Imagine a digital world without locks, alarms, or guards. That's what it would be like without cybersecurity. Cybersecurity is essentially the practice of protecting our computers, networks, and data from digital threats. Think of it as a shield against those who want to steal, damage, or disrupt our digital lives.

Why is Cybersecurity Important?

In today's world, we rely on technology for almost everything – from banking and shopping to communication and healthcare. This means our personal information, financial data, and even critical infrastructure are all vulnerable to cyberattacks.

Without cybersecurity, we risk:

- **Identity theft:** Hackers could steal your personal information and use it to open credit cards, file taxes fraudulently, or even apply for loans in your name.
- **Financial loss:** Cybercriminals could gain access to your bank accounts or online payment systems, draining your funds.
- **Data breaches:** Companies that store your data could be targeted, leading to the exposure of your sensitive

information like addresses, phone numbers, and even medical records.

- **Disruption of essential services:** Attacks on critical infrastructure, like power grids or hospitals, could disrupt vital services and put lives at risk.

Key Cybersecurity Concepts

To understand cybersecurity better, let's explore three core principles:

- **Confidentiality:** This is like keeping secrets. It ensures that only authorized individuals can access sensitive information. Think of strong passwords, encryption, and two-factor authentication as tools to maintain confidentiality.
- **Integrity:** This is about ensuring that data remains accurate and unchanged. Imagine someone tampering with your medical records or altering financial transactions. Integrity measures, like digital signatures and checksums, help prevent such unauthorized modifications.
- **Availability:** This ensures that systems and data are accessible when needed. Think of a denial-of-service attack that crashes a website or prevents you from accessing your online banking. Availability measures, like redundant systems and backups, help maintain continuous access.

Real-World Examples

Unfortunately, cyberattacks are becoming increasingly common. Here are a few examples that highlight the importance of cybersecurity:

- **The Equifax Data Breach (2017):** This massive data breach exposed the personal information of nearly 148 million people, highlighting the devastating consequences of inadequate security measures.
- **The NotPetya Ransomware Attack (2017):** This global cyberattack caused billions of dollars in damages by encrypting data and disrupting operations in various organizations, including hospitals and shipping companies.
- **The Colonial Pipeline Attack (2021):** This ransomware attack on a major US fuel pipeline caused widespread gas shortages and panic buying, demonstrating the vulnerability of critical infrastructure to cyber threats.

These examples show that cybersecurity is not just an IT issue; it's a societal issue that affects everyone. By understanding the basics of cybersecurity and taking necessary precautions, we can all contribute to a safer digital world.

CHAPTER 2: THE THREAT LANDSCAPE

Think of the digital world as a bustling city. In any city, there are always those who try to take advantage of others. In the digital world, these are our cyber threats.

Types of Cyber Threats

Here are some of the most common threats cybersecurity analysts face:

- **Malware:** This is malicious software designed to harm your computer or steal your data. Think of it like a digital virus. Different types of malware exist, including:
    - **Viruses:** These attach themselves to legitimate files and spread from one computer to another.
    - **Worms:** These are standalone programs that can self-replicate and spread across networks.
    - **Trojans:** These disguise themselves as harmless software but carry out malicious activities in the background.
    - **Ransomware:** This encrypts your files and demands a ransom to unlock them.
    - **Spyware:** This secretly monitors your activity and steals your information.

- **Phishing:** This involves tricking people into giving up their personal information. Imagine receiving an email that looks like it's from your bank, asking you to update your account details. That could be a phishing attempt.

- **Social Engineering:** This is a broader term that encompasses various psychological manipulation techniques to trick people into doing things that benefit the attacker. This could involve impersonation, pretexting (inventing a scenario), or baiting (offering something enticing).

- **Distributed Denial-of-Service (DDoS) Attacks:** Imagine a website being flooded with so much traffic that it crashes. That's a DDoS attack. Attackers use botnets (networks of infected computers) to overwhelm a target system, making it unavailable to legitimate users.

Motivations of Attackers

Cybercriminals have various motivations for launching attacks:

- **Financial gain:** Many attackers are motivated by money. They may steal credit card information, conduct online fraud, or demand ransoms.

- **Espionage:** Some attackers seek to steal sensitive information, like trade secrets or government intelligence.

- **Hacktivism:** These attackers are driven by political or social agendas. They may deface websites, leak confidential data, or disrupt online services to make a statement.

Real-World Examples

- **The WannaCry Ransomware Attack (2017):** This global attack affected hundreds of thousands of computers, encrypting their data and demanding a ransom in Bitcoin. It crippled hospitals, businesses, and government agencies worldwide.
- **The SolarWinds Supply Chain Attack (2020):** This sophisticated attack compromised the software update mechanism of SolarWinds, a popular IT management platform. This allowed attackers to gain access to the networks of thousands of organizations, including government agencies and Fortune 500 companies.

These examples demonstrate the diverse nature of cyber threats and the potential for significant damage. By understanding the threat landscape and the motivations of attackers, cybersecurity analysts can better prepare for and respond to these challenges.

CHAPTER 3: CYBERSECURITY FRAMEWORKS AND STANDARDS

Imagine building a house without blueprints or following any building codes. It would be chaotic, and the result would likely be unstable and unsafe. Similarly, in cybersecurity, we need frameworks and standards to guide us in building secure systems and processes.

What are Cybersecurity Frameworks and Standards?

Cybersecurity frameworks and standards are essentially sets of guidelines, best practices, and recommendations that organizations can adopt to manage and mitigate cyber risks. They provide a structured approach to cybersecurity, helping organizations:

- **Identify and assess risks:** Frameworks help organizations understand their vulnerabilities and the potential impact of cyberattacks.
- **Implement security controls:** They provide guidance on selecting and implementing appropriate security measures to protect against threats.

- **Monitor and improve security posture:** Frameworks help organizations continuously monitor their security posture and make improvements over time.
- **Comply with regulations:** Many industries have specific cybersecurity regulations that organizations must adhere to, and frameworks can help them achieve compliance.

Key Cybersecurity Frameworks and Standards

Let's explore some of the most widely recognized frameworks and standards:

- **NIST Cybersecurity Framework (CSF)**

  Developed by the National Institute of Standards and Technology (NIST) in the US, the CSF is a voluntary framework that provides a set of standards, guidelines, and best practices to manage cybersecurity risks. It's widely adopted across various sectors and is designed to be flexible and adaptable to different organizational needs.

  The CSF consists of five core functions:

  1. **Identify:** Develop an organizational understanding to manage cybersecurity risk to systems, assets, data, and capabilities.
  2. **Protect:** Develop and implement the appropriate safeguards to ensure appropriate activities to

identify the occurrence of a cybersecurity event. appropriate activities to maintain plans for resilience and to restore any capabilities or services that were impaired due to a cybersecurity event.

These functions are further broken down into categories and subcategories, providing a comprehensive roadmap for managing cybersecurity risks.

- **ISO 27001**

ISO/IEC 27001 is an internationally recognized standard for information security management systems (ISMS). It provides a framework for establishing, implementing, maintaining, and continually improving an ISMS. The standard emphasizes a risk-based approach, requiring organizations to identify their information security risks and implement appropriate controls to mitigate them. ISO 27001 certification demonstrates an organization's commitment to information security and can provide a competitive advantage.

- **CIS Controls**

The Center for Internet Security (CIS) Controls are a set of prioritized security controls designed to protect against the most common cyberattacks. They are developed through a consensus process involving cybersecurity experts from around the world. The CIS Controls are organized into three Implementation Groups (IGs) based on the organization's cybersecurity maturity:

1. **IG1:** Basic cyber hygiene for all organizations.
2. **IG2:** Intermediate protections for organizations with more sensitive data or higher risk profiles.
3. **IG3:** Advanced protections for organizations with critical assets or facing sophisticated threats.

By implementing the CIS Controls, organizations can significantly reduce their risk of cyberattacks.

Importance of Compliance and Industry Best Practices

Compliance with cybersecurity frameworks, standards, and regulations is crucial for several reasons:

- **Protecting sensitive data:** Compliance helps organizations protect sensitive data, such as customer information, financial records, and intellectual property.
- **Maintaining customer trust:** Demonstrating compliance with security standards can help build trust with customers and stakeholders.

- **Avoiding penalties and legal issues:** Non-compliance with regulations can result in hefty fines and legal repercussions.
- **Improving security posture:** Following industry best practices can help organizations improve their overall security posture and reduce their risk of cyberattacks.

Real-World Examples

- **General Data Protection Regulation (GDPR)**

  GDPR is a comprehensive data protection regulation in the European Union (EU) that sets strict requirements for the processing of personal data. Organizations that handle the personal data of EU residents must comply with GDPR, regardless of their location. GDPR mandates various security measures, including data encryption, access controls, and data breach notification protocols.

- **Health Insurance Portability and Accountability Act (HIPAA)**

  HIPAA is a US federal law that sets standards for the protection of sensitive patient health information. Healthcare organizations must comply with HIPAA to safeguard patient privacy and confidentiality. HIPAA requires implementing various security measures, including access controls, audit trails, and data encryption.

- **Payment Card Industry Data Security Standard (PCI DSS)**

  PCI DSS is a set of security standards designed to protect credit card data. Merchants and service providers that process credit card payments must comply with PCI DSS to prevent data breaches and fraud. PCI DSS mandates various security controls, including network segmentation, access controls, and regular security assessments.

Cybersecurity frameworks and standards provide essential guidance for organizations to build robust security programs. By adopting these frameworks and complying with relevant regulations, organizations can protect their sensitive data, maintain customer trust, and reduce their risk of cyberattacks.

This chapter provides a comprehensive overview of cybersecurity frameworks and standards, highlighting their importance in building a strong security posture. Remember to use real-world examples and case studies throughout the book to illustrate the practical application of these concepts.

Sources and related content

CHAPTER 4: NETWORK SECURITY FUNDAMENTALS

Think of a network like a highway system. Data packets are like cars traveling between different destinations. Just as we have rules and infrastructure to manage traffic flow and ensure safety on highways, we need mechanisms to protect our networks and the data flowing through them. This is where network security comes in.

Network Topologies, Protocols, and Devices

Before we dive into security measures, let's understand some basic network concepts:

- **Network Topologies:** This refers to the arrangement of different elements (like computers, servers, and other devices) in a network. Common topologies include:
    - **Bus Topology:** All devices are connected to a single cable.
    - **Star Topology:** All devices are connected to a central hub or switch.
    - **Ring Topology:** Devices are connected in a circular chain.

o **Mesh Topology:** Devices are interconnected with multiple paths.

- **Network Protocols:** These are sets of rules that govern how data is transmitted over a network. Think of them as the language that devices use to communicate with each other. Some key protocols include:

  o **TCP/IP:** This suite of protocols forms the foundation of the internet.

  o **HTTP:** This protocol is used for transferring web pages.

  o **HTTPS:** This is the secure version of HTTP, which encrypts data to protect it from eavesdropping.

  o **DNS:** This protocol translates domain names (like [invalid URL removed]) into IP addresses.

- **Network Devices:** These are the hardware components that make up a network. Some common devices include:

  o **Routers:** These direct traffic between different networks.

  o **Switches:** These connect devices within a network.

  o **Firewalls:** These filter network traffic based on predefined rules.

  o **Intrusion Detection Systems (IDSs):** These monitor network traffic for suspicious activity.

Firewalls: The Gatekeepers of Network Security

Imagine a castle with a strong wall and a gate guarded by vigilant soldiers. That's what a firewall does for your network. It acts as a barrier between your internal network and the outside world, controlling the flow of traffic based on predefined rules.

How Firewalls Work

Firewalls examine incoming and outgoing network traffic and block any traffic that doesn't meet the specified security criteria. They can filter traffic based on various factors, such as:

- **Source and destination IP addresses:** Firewalls can block traffic from specific IP addresses or ranges.
- **Port numbers:** They can block or allow traffic on specific ports. For example, they might block incoming traffic on port 23 (Telnet) to prevent unauthorized remote access.
- **Protocols:** Firewalls can block traffic using specific protocols, like blocking all FTP traffic.
- **Content filtering:** Some firewalls can examine the content of data packets to block malicious content or prevent data leakage.

Types of Firewalls

- **Packet filtering firewalls:** These examine individual data packets and make decisions based on the packet header information.

- **Stateful inspection firewalls:** These keep track of the state of network connections and make decisions based on the context of the connection.

- **Application-level firewalls:** These operate at the application layer and can filter traffic based on the application being used.

- **Next-generation firewalls (NGFWs):** These combine traditional firewall capabilities with advanced features like intrusion prevention and malware scanning.

Real-World Example: How a Firewall Prevents Unauthorized Access

Let's say a hacker tries to access your computer remotely by trying to connect to a specific port that's used for remote access. If you have a firewall configured to block incoming connections on that port, the firewall will prevent the hacker from accessing your computer.

Intrusion Detection Systems (IDSs): The Network Watchdogs

While firewalls act as a first line of defense, intrusion detection systems (IDSs) provide an additional layer of security by monitoring network traffic for suspicious activity. Think of them as security cameras that constantly scan for any signs of trouble.

How IDSs Work

IDSs analyze network traffic for patterns that match known attack signatures or deviate from normal behavior. They can detect various types of attacks, including:

- **Malware activity:** IDSs can identify traffic patterns associated with malware infections.
- **Port scans:** They can detect attempts to scan your network for open ports that could be exploited.
- **Denial-of-service attacks:** IDSs can identify unusual traffic spikes that might indicate a DDoS attack.
- **Unauthorized access attempts:** They can detect attempts to access restricted resources or data.

Types of IDSs

- **Network-based IDSs (NIDSs):** These monitor traffic on the entire network.
- **Host-based IDSs (HIDSs):** These monitor activity on a specific host or device.

Real-World Example: Detecting a Malware Infection

If a computer on your network becomes infected with malware that tries to communicate with a command-and-control server, an IDS could detect this suspicious communication pattern and alert security personnel.

Virtual Private Networks (VPNs): Secure Tunnels Through the Internet

Imagine needing to send a confidential document across a crowded room. You might put it in a sealed envelope to protect it from prying eyes. That's what a VPN does for your data. It creates a secure, encrypted tunnel through the internet, protecting your data from eavesdropping and interception.

How VPNs Work

When you connect to a VPN, your internet traffic is routed through an encrypted tunnel to a VPN server. This means that:

- Your data is encrypted, making it unreadable to anyone who might intercept it.
- Your IP address is masked, making it appear as if you're browsing from the location of the VPN server.

Uses of VPNs

- **Secure remote access:** Employees can use VPNs to securely access company resources from anywhere.
- **Protecting sensitive data:** VPNs can be used to protect sensitive data when using public Wi-Fi networks.
- **Bypassing geo-restrictions:** VPNs can be used to access websites or services that are blocked in certain regions.

Real-World Example: How a VPN Encrypts Data

Let's say you're using a public Wi-Fi network at a coffee shop. If you connect to a VPN, your internet traffic will be encrypted, preventing anyone on the same network from snooping on your online activity.

Conclusion

Network security is a critical aspect of cybersecurity, and understanding the fundamentals is crucial for any aspiring analyst. By implementing security measures like firewalls, IDSs, and VPNs, organizations can protect their networks and data from a wide range of cyber threats.

CHAPTER 5: OPERATING SYSTEMS AND SECURITY

Operating systems are the foundation upon which our digital world is built. They manage the hardware and software resources of a computer system, providing a platform for applications to run and users to interact with the machine. But operating systems also play a critical role in cybersecurity, as they provide built-in security features and mechanisms to protect against threats.

Windows, Linux, macOS Security Features

Each operating system has its own set of security features, but some common ones include:

- **User Account Control (UAC):** This feature helps prevent unauthorized changes to the system by prompting users for confirmation before performing actions that require administrator privileges.
- **Firewall:** A built-in firewall filters network traffic and blocks unauthorized connections.
- **Antivirus Software:** Many operating systems come with built-in antivirus software or offer it as an optional installation.

- **Disk Encryption:** This feature encrypts the entire hard drive, protecting data even if the device is lost or stolen.
- **Secure Boot:** This feature ensures that only trusted software is loaded during the boot process, preventing malware from hijacking the system.

Windows Security Features

Windows, being the most widely used desktop operating system, offers a comprehensive suite of security features:

- **Windows Defender:** This built-in security suite includes antivirus, firewall, and intrusion prevention capabilities.
- **BitLocker:** This feature provides full disk encryption, protecting data at rest.
- **Windows Hello:** This biometric authentication feature allows users to log in using facial recognition or fingerprint scanning.
- **AppLocker:** This feature allows administrators to control which applications users can run, preventing the execution of unauthorized software.

Linux Security Features

Linux, known for its open-source nature and stability, also boasts strong security features:

- **iptables:** This powerful firewall allows granular control over network traffic.

- **AppArmor and SELinux:** These security modules provide mandatory access control, restricting what applications can do and access.

- **chroot:** This command allows administrators to create a restricted environment for applications, limiting their access to the rest of the system.

- **sudo:** This command allows users to execute commands with elevated privileges without logging in as the root user.

macOS Security Features

macOS, built on a Unix foundation, inherits many security features from its predecessor:

- **Gatekeeper:** This feature prevents users from installing applications from untrusted sources.

- **XProtect:** This built-in anti-malware software scans for and removes known malware.

- **FileVault:** This feature provides full disk encryption, protecting data at rest.

- **System Integrity Protection (SIP):** This feature prevents even root users from modifying critical system files and directories.

User Account Management

Proper user account management is essential for maintaining a secure system. This involves:

- **Creating strong passwords:** Passwords should be long, complex, and unique.
- **Implementing password policies:** Enforce password complexity requirements and regular password changes.
- **Using multi-factor authentication (MFA):** MFA adds an extra layer of security by requiring users to provide multiple forms of authentication, such as a password and a one-time code.
- **Assigning appropriate privileges:** Users should only have the necessary permissions to perform their job duties.
- **Regularly reviewing and auditing user accounts:** Inactive or unnecessary accounts should be disabled or deleted.

Access Control

Access control mechanisms regulate who can access what resources on a system. This involves:

- **Authentication:** Verifying the identity of users before granting access.
- **Authorization:** Determining what actions users are allowed to perform.

- **Access control lists (ACLs):** Defining rules for which users or groups have access to specific files or directories.
- **Role-based access control (RBAC):** Assigning permissions based on roles within an organization.

Security Hardening

Security hardening involves taking steps to make a system more secure by reducing its attack surface. This can include:

- **Disabling unnecessary services and features:** Remove any software or services that are not needed.
- **Applying security updates and patches:** Keep the operating system and applications up to date with the latest security fixes.
- **Configuring security settings:** Adjust system settings to enhance security, such as disabling guest accounts and enabling firewall protection.
- **Implementing logging and auditing:** Track system events and user activity to detect suspicious behavior.

Real-World Examples

- **Setting up strong passwords:** Use a combination of uppercase and lowercase letters, numbers, and symbols. Avoid using common words or personal information in passwords. Consider using a password manager to generate and store strong passwords.

- **Implementing multi-factor authentication:** Enable MFA for all critical accounts, such as email, banking, and social media. Use authenticator apps or hardware tokens for stronger security.

- **Regularly updating software:** Enable automatic updates for the operating system and applications. Regularly check for and install security patches.

Operating systems play a vital role in cybersecurity, providing built-in security features and mechanisms to protect against threats. By understanding the security features of different operating systems, implementing proper user account management, and employing access control and security hardening techniques, organizations can significantly strengthen their security posture.

CHAPTER 6: CYBERSECURITY TOOLS AND TECHNOLOGIES

In the ongoing battle against cyber threats, cybersecurity analysts rely on a diverse arsenal of tools and technologies. These tools help them detect, analyze, and respond to security incidents, strengthen defenses, and stay one step ahead of attackers. This chapter explores some of the essential tools and technologies in a cybersecurity analyst's toolkit.

Security Information and Event Management (SIEM) Systems

Imagine trying to find a needle in a haystack. That's what it can be like to sift through mountains of security logs and alerts to identify potential threats. SIEM systems help automate this process, providing a centralized platform for collecting, analyzing, and monitoring security events from various sources across an organization's IT infrastructure.

How SIEM Systems Work

SIEM systems collect log data from various sources, such as firewalls, intrusion detection systems, servers, and applications. They then use correlation rules and machine learning algorithms to analyze this data in real-time, identifying patterns and anomalies that might indicate a security incident. SIEM systems can also generate alerts, trigger automated responses, and provide dashboards and reports for security monitoring and analysis.

Key Features of SIEM Systems

- **Log Management:** Collects and stores security logs from various sources.
- **Correlation and Analysis:** Analyzes log data to identify security events and patterns.
- **Alerting:** Generates alerts based on predefined rules or anomalies.
- **Dashboards and Reporting:** Provides visualizations and reports for security monitoring and analysis.
- **Incident Response:** Helps with incident investigation and response.

Real-World Example: Splunk

Splunk is a popular SIEM platform that provides real-time visibility into security events across an organization's IT environment. It can ingest data from various sources, analyze it using powerful search and reporting capabilities, and generate alerts based on predefined rules or machine learning models. Splunk also offers dashboards and visualizations to help security analysts understand and respond to threats effectively.

Vulnerability Scanners

Think of a vulnerability scanner as a security checkup for your IT systems. These tools automatically scan networks and applications for known vulnerabilities, helping organizations identify weaknesses that could be exploited by attackers.

How Vulnerability Scanners Work

Vulnerability scanners use a database of known vulnerabilities and exploit techniques to test systems for potential weaknesses. They can scan various assets, including:

- **Network devices:** Routers, switches, firewalls.
- **Servers:** Web servers, database servers, mail servers.
- **Applications:** Web applications, mobile applications, desktop applications.

Key Features of Vulnerability Scanners

- **Comprehensive Vulnerability Database:** Includes a wide range of known vulnerabilities.
- **Automated Scanning:** Regularly scans systems for vulnerabilities.
- **Prioritized Reporting:** Ranks vulnerabilities based on severity and provides recommendations for remediation.
- **Integration with other security tools:** Can integrate with SIEM systems and other security tools for a holistic view of security posture.

Real-World Example: Nessus

Nessus is a widely used vulnerability scanner that offers a comprehensive vulnerability database and powerful scanning capabilities. It can identify a wide range of vulnerabilities, including missing patches, misconfigurations, and coding errors. Nessus also provides detailed reports with remediation recommendations, helping organizations prioritize and address security weaknesses.

Penetration Testing Tools

Penetration testing, or ethical hacking, involves simulating real-world attacks to identify vulnerabilities in systems and applications. Penetration testing tools provide cybersecurity professionals with the tools they need to conduct these assessments.

Types of Penetration Testing Tools

- **Network Scanners:** Used to discover devices and services on a network.
- **Vulnerability Scanners:** Used to identify known vulnerabilities in systems and applications.
- **Exploit Frameworks:** Used to exploit vulnerabilities and gain access to systems.
- **Password Cracking Tools:** Used to test the strength of passwords.
- **Wireless Testing Tools:** Used to assess the security of wireless networks.

Real-World Example: Metasploit

Metasploit is a popular penetration testing framework that provides a vast collection of exploits, payloads, and tools for conducting security assessments. It allows security professionals to simulate various attack scenarios, identify vulnerabilities, and test the effectiveness of security controls.

Other Essential Cybersecurity Tools and Technologies

In addition to the tools mentioned above, cybersecurity analysts utilize a variety of other technologies:

- **Network Protocol Analyzers:** These tools capture and analyze network traffic, helping identify malicious activity and troubleshoot network issues. Wireshark is a popular example.
- **Forensic Tools:** These tools are used to investigate security incidents and gather evidence. Autopsy and The Sleuth Kit are commonly used for digital forensics.
- **Encryption Tools:** These tools are used to protect data confidentiality and integrity. OpenSSL and GnuPG are popular examples.
- **Anti-malware Tools:** These tools detect and remove malware from systems. Popular examples include Malwarebytes and Kaspersky.

- **Security Information and Event Management (SIEM) Systems:** These tools collect and analyze security logs from various sources, providing real-time visibility into security events. Splunk and IBM QRadar are popular SIEM solutions.

- **Intrusion Detection and Prevention Systems (IDPS):** These tools monitor network traffic for suspicious activity and can block or alert on potential threats. Snort and Suricata are popular open-source IDPS solutions.

- **Endpoint Detection and Response (EDR) Tools:** These tools monitor endpoints (computers and mobile devices) for malicious activity and can provide detailed information about attacks. CrowdStrike and Carbon Black are popular EDR solutions.

- **Threat Intelligence Platforms:** These platforms provide curated threat intelligence data that can be used to identify and respond to emerging threats. Recorded Future and ThreatConnect are popular threat intelligence platforms.

Cybersecurity tools and technologies play a crucial role in enabling analysts to defend against an ever-evolving threat landscape. By utilizing a combination of these tools, cybersecurity professionals can strengthen defenses, detect and respond to security incidents effectively, and protect critical assets from cyberattacks.

CHAPTER 7: THREAT INTELLIGENCE AND ANALYSIS

In the ever-evolving landscape of cyber threats, staying ahead of the curve is crucial. Threat intelligence provides the knowledge and insights needed to proactively defend against attacks, mitigate risks, and make informed security decisions.

What is Threat Intelligence?

Threat intelligence is essentially evidence-based knowledge about existing or emerging threats. It's like having a crystal ball that helps you see what's coming and prepare accordingly. This knowledge can include information about:

- **Threat actors:** Who are the attackers? What are their motivations and capabilities?
- **Attack methods:** What tactics, techniques, and procedures (TTPs) do they use?
- **Vulnerabilities:** What weaknesses in systems and applications are they exploiting?
- **Indicators of compromise (IOCs):** What are the telltale signs of an attack?

Sources of Threat Intelligence

Threat intelligence can be gathered from various sources:

- **Open-source intelligence (OSINT):** This refers to publicly available information that can be gathered from sources like:
    - Security blogs and news sites
    - Social media
    - Online forums and communities
    - Academic research papers
    - Vulnerability databases (e.g., CVE)
    - Threat intelligence platforms (e.g., VirusTotal)
- **Commercial threat intelligence:** This refers to intelligence gathered and analyzed by specialized security vendors. These vendors often have access to proprietary data sources and advanced analytics capabilities, providing more in-depth and actionable intelligence.
- **Government threat intelligence:** Government agencies, like the Cybersecurity and Infrastructure Security Agency (CISA) in the US, collect and share threat intelligence to help protect critical infrastructure and national security.

Analyzing Threat Data to Identify Potential Attacks

Gathering threat intelligence is only the first step. The real value lies in analyzing this data to identify potential attacks and proactively defend against them. This involves:

- **Data collection:** Gathering threat data from various sources.

- **Data processing:** Cleaning, normalizing, and structuring the data for analysis.

- **Data analysis:** Applying analytical techniques to identify patterns, trends, and anomalies.

- **Threat assessment:** Evaluating the credibility and potential impact of threats.

- **Dissemination:** Sharing threat intelligence with relevant stakeholders.

Real-World Examples

- **Using VirusTotal to analyze malware:** VirusTotal is a free online service that allows you to analyze files and URLs to detect malware. You can upload a suspicious file or enter a URL, and VirusTotal will scan it with multiple antivirus engines and provide a report on its findings. This can help you determine if a file is malicious and understand its potential impact.

- **Following security blogs and news sites:** Staying up-to-date on the latest security news and trends is crucial for threat intelligence analysis. Security blogs and news sites often report on new vulnerabilities, attack methods, and threat actors. By following these sources, you can stay informed about emerging threats and proactively defend against them.

Benefits of Threat Intelligence

- **Proactive defense:** Anticipate and mitigate threats before they cause damage.
- **Improved incident response:** Respond to security incidents more quickly and effectively.
- **Reduced risk:** Make informed security decisions based on threat intelligence.
- **Enhanced situational awareness:** Gain a better understanding of the threat landscape.
- **Increased efficiency:** Automate security tasks and focus on high-priority threats.

Threat intelligence is a critical component of a robust cybersecurity strategy. [1] By gathering, analyzing, and sharing threat intelligence, organizations can proactively defend against attacks, mitigate risks, and stay ahead of the curve in the ever-evolving cyber threat landscape. [2]

CHAPTER 8: INCIDENT RESPONSE

Imagine a fire breaking out in a building. You wouldn't just stand there and watch; you'd have a plan to extinguish the flames, evacuate people safely, and assess the damage. Similarly, in cybersecurity, incident response is the process of dealing with security incidents, minimizing damage, and restoring normal operations.

Incident Response Lifecycle

The incident response lifecycle is a structured approach to handling security incidents. It typically involves the following phases:

1. **Preparation:** This phase involves getting ready for potential incidents. It includes:
   o   Establishing an incident response team
   o   Developing an incident response plan
   o   Conducting training and exercises
   o   Implementing security controls and monitoring tools
2. **Detection:** This phase involves identifying and confirming security incidents. It might involve:
   o   Monitoring security alerts
   o   Analyzing logs and network traffic
   o   Receiving reports from users or security tools

3. **Analysis:** This phase involves investigating the incident to understand its scope, impact, and root cause. It might include:
   - Gathering evidence
   - Analyzing malware
   - Tracing attack vectors

4. **Containment:** This phase involves limiting the damage and preventing the incident from spreading. It might include:
   - Isolating affected systems
   - Blocking malicious traffic
   - Changing passwords

5. **Eradication:** This phase involves removing the root cause of the incident. It might include:
   - Removing malware
   - Patching vulnerabilities
   - Rebuilding compromised systems

6. **Recovery:** This phase involves restoring normal operations. It might include:
   - Restoring data from backups
   - Rebuilding systems
   - Testing and validating systems

Developing an Incident Response Plan

An incident response plan is a documented guide that outlines the steps to take in case of a security incident. It should include:

- **Incident response team roles and responsibilities**
- **Incident reporting and escalation procedures**
- **Incident classification and severity levels**
- **Containment and eradication strategies**
- **Recovery procedures**
- **Communication plan**
- **Post-incident activities (e.g., lessons learned)**

Real-World Examples

- **Responding to a phishing attack:**
    - Detect: A user reports receiving a suspicious email.
    - Analyze: The incident response team analyzes the email and determines it's a phishing attempt.
    - Contain: The team blocks the sender's email address and warns other users about the phishing campaign.
    - Eradicate: The team scans the user's computer for malware and removes any infections.
    - Recover: The team educates the user about phishing attacks and reinforces security awareness training.
- **Recovering from a ransomware infection:**
    - Detect: Users report that their files are encrypted and they cannot access them.

- o Analyze: The incident response team confirms a ransomware infection and identifies the ransomware variant.
- o Contain: The team isolates affected systems to prevent further spread.
- o Eradicate: The team removes the ransomware and restores data from backups.
- o Recover: The team rebuilds compromised systems and implements stronger security controls to prevent future infections.

Key Takeaways

- Incident response is a crucial process for managing and mitigating security incidents.
- The incident response lifecycle provides a structured approach to handling incidents.
- A well-defined incident response plan is essential for effective incident response.
- Real-world examples illustrate how incident response can be applied to different types of security incidents.

By following the incident response lifecycle and having a solid incident response plan, organizations can minimize the impact of security incidents, recover quickly, and strengthen their overall security posture.

CHAPTER 9: CLOUD SECURITY

Cloud computing has revolutionized the way we use technology, offering scalability, flexibility, and cost-effectiveness. But with these benefits come new security challenges. Cloud security focuses on protecting data, applications, and infrastructure in the cloud.

Securing Cloud Environments (AWS, Azure, GCP)

The major cloud providers—Amazon Web Services (AWS), Microsoft Azure, and Google Cloud Platform (GCP)—offer a range of security tools and services to help organizations secure their cloud environments.

AWS Security Features:

- **AWS Identity and Access Management (IAM):** This service allows you to manage users, groups, and permissions, controlling who can access what resources in your AWS account.
- **AWS Security Groups:** These act as virtual firewalls for your EC2 instances, controlling inbound and outbound traffic.

- **AWS Key Management Service (KMS):** This service allows you to create and manage encryption keys, protecting your data at rest and in transit.
- **Amazon GuardDuty:** This threat detection service uses machine learning to identify malicious activity in your AWS account.

Azure Security Features:

- **Azure Active Directory (Azure AD):** This identity and access management service allows you to manage users, groups, and permissions in your Azure environment.
- **Azure Firewall:** This cloud-native firewall service protects your Azure resources from network threats.
- **Azure Key Vault:** This service allows you to securely store and manage secrets, such as passwords, API keys, and certificates.
- **Azure Security Center:** This unified security management system provides threat protection and security posture management across your hybrid cloud workloads.

GCP Security Features:

- **Cloud Identity and Access Management (Cloud IAM):** This service allows you to manage users, groups, and permissions in your GCP environment.

- **Cloud Firewall:** This network firewall allows you to control traffic to and from your GCP resources.

- **Cloud Key Management Service (Cloud KMS):** This service allows you to create and manage encryption keys for your data.

- **Security Command Center:** This security and data risk platform helps you prevent, detect, and respond to threats across your GCP resources.

Cloud Security Best Practices

Regardless of which cloud provider you choose, there are some best practices that apply across the board:

- **Understand the Shared Responsibility Model:** Cloud security is a shared responsibility between the cloud provider and the customer. The provider is responsible for securing the underlying infrastructure, while the customer is responsible for securing their own data and applications.

- **Implement Strong Identity and Access Management:** Control who can access your cloud resources by implementing strong authentication and authorization mechanisms.

- **Encrypt Your Data:** Protect your data at rest and in transit using encryption.

- **Regularly Monitor and Audit Your Cloud Environment:** Use monitoring tools and conduct regular security audits to identify and address potential vulnerabilities.
- **Implement a Disaster Recovery Plan:** Have a plan in place to recover your data and applications in case of a disaster or outage.

Real-World Examples

- **Securing data in Amazon S3:** You can encrypt data stored in Amazon S3 using server-side encryption with Amazon S3-managed keys (SSE-S3), server-side encryption with customer-provided keys (SSE-C), or server-side encryption with AWS KMS-managed keys (SSE-KMS). You can also implement access controls using bucket policies and access control lists (ACLs).
- **Implementing access controls in Azure Active Directory:** You can use Azure AD to manage user access to your Azure resources. You can create users, groups, and roles, and assign permissions based on their job responsibilities. You can also implement multi-factor authentication (MFA) for added security.

Cloud security is a critical aspect of cybersecurity in today's cloud-centric world. By understanding the security features offered by different cloud providers, implementing security best practices, and following real-world examples, organizations can secure their cloud environments and protect their valuable data and applications.

CHAPTER 10: DATA SECURITY AND PRIVACY

Data is a valuable asset for any organization, and protecting it is paramount. Data security involves implementing measures to safeguard data from unauthorized access, use, disclosure, disruption, modification, or destruction. Privacy, on the other hand, focuses on the ethical and legal obligations to protect personal information and respect individual rights.

Data Encryption

Encryption is a fundamental technique for protecting data confidentiality and integrity. It involves converting data into a scrambled format (ciphertext) that can only be deciphered with the appropriate decryption key. This ensures that even if unauthorized individuals gain access to the data, they cannot understand or use it.

- **Types of Encryption:**
  - **Symmetric encryption:** Uses the same key for encryption and decryption.

- o **Asymmetric encryption:** Uses a pair of keys—a public key for encryption and a private key for decryption.
- **Encryption Algorithms:**
  - o **AES (Advanced Encryption Standard):** A widely used symmetric encryption algorithm, available in different key lengths (e.g., AES-256).
  - o **RSA:** A widely used asymmetric encryption algorithm.

Real-World Example: Encrypting Sensitive Data with AES-256

To protect sensitive data like customer credit card information, a company can use AES-256 to encrypt the data before storing it in their database. This ensures that even if the database is compromised, the attackers cannot access the sensitive information without the decryption key.

Data Loss Prevention (DLP)

DLP focuses on preventing sensitive data from leaving the organization's control. It involves implementing tools and policies to detect, monitor, and block the unauthorized transmission of sensitive data.

- **DLP Techniques:**

- o **Network DLP:** Monitors network traffic for sensitive data.
  - o **Endpoint DLP:** Monitors endpoints (computers and mobile devices) for sensitive data.
  - o **Data at rest DLP:** Scans data stored in databases and file systems for sensitive data.
- **DLP Tools:**
  - o **Forcepoint DLP**
  - o **Symantec DLP**
  - o **McAfee DLP**

Privacy Regulations

Various privacy regulations around the world mandate how organizations must handle personal information. Two prominent examples are:

- **General Data Protection Regulation (GDPR):** This EU regulation sets strict requirements for the processing of personal data of EU residents, emphasizing data protection principles like data minimization, purpose limitation, and data accuracy.
- **California Consumer Privacy Act (CCPA):** This California law grants consumers various rights regarding their personal information, including the right to know what information is collected, the right to delete their

information, and the right to opt-out of the sale of their information.

Real-World Example: Implementing Data Masking Techniques

To protect sensitive data like Social Security numbers, a company can implement data masking techniques. This involves replacing sensitive data with fictional data that retains the format and characteristics of the original data but does not reveal the actual sensitive information. This allows the company to share data for testing or development purposes without compromising privacy.

Data security and privacy are essential aspects of cybersecurity. By implementing data encryption, data loss prevention techniques, and complying with privacy regulations, organizati

CHAPTER 11: APPLICATION SECURITY

Application security focuses on protecting software applications from threats throughout their lifecycle. It involves a combination of secure coding practices, security testing, and ongoing monitoring to prevent vulnerabilities and mitigate risks.

Secure Coding Practices

Writing secure code is the first line of defense against application vulnerabilities. Developers should follow secure coding practices to minimize security risks from the start. This includes:

- **Input validation:** Validate all user input to prevent injection attacks.
- **Output encoding:** Encode output to prevent cross-site scripting (XSS) vulnerabilities.
- **Authentication and authorization:** Implement strong authentication and authorization mechanisms to control access to application resources.
- **Session management:** Securely manage user sessions to prevent session hijacking and fixation.

- **Error handling:** Handle errors gracefully to avoid revealing sensitive information.
- **Logging and auditing:** Log security-related events and user activity for monitoring and incident response.
- **Use of secure libraries and frameworks:** Leverage well-vetted libraries and frameworks to avoid introducing known vulnerabilities.

Vulnerability Assessment

Vulnerability assessment involves identifying and prioritizing security weaknesses in applications. This can be done through:

- **Static analysis:** Analyzing source code for potential vulnerabilities.
- **Dynamic analysis:** Testing the running application for vulnerabilities.
- **Software Composition Analysis (SCA):** Identifying known vulnerabilities in open-source components used in the application.

Penetration Testing

Penetration testing, or ethical hacking, involves simulating real-world attacks to identify vulnerabilities in applications. This can help uncover weaknesses that might be missed by automated vulnerability scanners.

OWASP Top 10 Web Application Vulnerabilities

The Open Web Application Security Project (OWASP) Top 10 is a globally recognized standard awareness document for web application security. It lists the ten most critical web application security risks:

1. **Broken Access Control:** Restricting access to authorized users only.
2. **Cryptographic Failures:** Protecting data with strong encryption.
3. **Injection:** Preventing injection attacks like SQL injection and cross-site scripting (XSS).
4. **Insecure Design:** Designing applications with security in mind from the start.
5. **Security Misconfiguration:** Properly configuring security settings.
6. **Vulnerable and Outdated Components:** Using up-to-date and secure components.
7. **Identification and Authentication Failures:** Implementing strong authentication mechanisms.
8. **Software and Data Integrity Failures:** Ensuring software and data integrity.
9. **Security Logging and Monitoring Failures:** Logging security events and monitoring for suspicious activity.

10. **Server-Side Request Forgery (SSRF):** Preventing SSRF attacks that exploit applications to access internal resources.

Real-World Examples

- **SQL Injection Attacks:** Attackers can inject malicious SQL code into input fields to manipulate database queries, potentially gaining unauthorized access to data or even taking control of the database server.
- **Cross-site Scripting (XSS):** Attackers can inject malicious scripts into web pages viewed by other users. These scripts can then steal user data, hijack sessions, or redirect users to malicious websites.

Application security is a critical aspect of cybersecurity. By following secure coding practices, conducting vulnerability assessments and penetration testing, and staying informed about common web application vulnerabilities like the OWASP Top 10, developers can create more secure applications and protect users from cyber threats.

Shell scripting is a powerful way to automate repetitive tasks and streamline workflows on Linux. A shell script is simply a text file containing a sequence of commands that the shell executes as a program. By creating scripts, you can automate common tasks such as organizing files, performing backups, managing system resources, and even creating complex workflows for development.

Shell scripts are written in shell languages like **Bash** (Bourne Again SHell), which is the default on most Linux distributions. A shell script typically includes:

- **Commands**: A sequence of shell commands that are executed in order.
- **Variables**: For storing and reusing values.
- **Control structures**: Logic like loops (for, while) and conditional statements (if, else) to make scripts more dynamic and responsive to different situations.

The Basics of Writing a Shell Script

1. **Creating a New Script File**
   - To write a shell script, start by creating a new text file with the .sh extension. For example:

   bash
   Copy code
   nano my_script.sh

   - In the file, start by adding the **shebang** (#!) line at the top, which tells the shell which interpreter to use. For Bash, the line is:

bash

Copy code

#!/bin/bash

o   This line ensures that the script runs in the Bash shell, regardless of which shell you are using.

2. **Adding Commands to the Script**

o   After the shebang, you can add any commands you want the script to execute. For example:

bash

Copy code

#!/bin/bash

echo "Hello, World!"

o   This script simply prints "Hello, World!" to the terminal. Save the file and close the editor.

3. **Making the Script Executable**

o   To run a shell script, you need to make it executable. Use the chmod command to grant execute permissions:

bash

Copy code

chmod +x my_script.sh

o   Now, you can execute the script by typing:

```
bash
Copy code
./my_script.sh
```

- o The output will display Hello, World!, showing that the script executed successfully.

4. **Using Variables in Shell Scripts**
    - o Variables allow you to store values and reuse them in your script. In a shell script, you can assign a value to a variable without spaces around the = sign:

```bash
Copy code
#!/bin/bash
name="Alice"
echo "Hello, $name!"
```

- o Here, $name refers to the value stored in name. When you run this script, it will print Hello, Alice!.

5. **Adding Conditional Statements and Loops**
    - o Shell scripts support control structures like conditional statements and loops to perform tasks based on certain conditions or to repeat tasks multiple times.
    - o For example, using a loop to print numbers from 1 to 5:

```
bash
Copy code
#!/bin/bash
for i in {1..5}
do
  echo "Number: $i"
done
```

o   This script prints each number from 1 to 5.

Example: Automating Repetitive Tasks like Organizing Files or Performing Backups

Let's walk through a practical example where you create a shell script to organize files and back up important documents. In this example, you'll write a script that:

1. **Organizes files by file type** into separate directories (e.g., moves .txt files into a TextFiles directory and .jpg files into an Images directory).
2. **Creates a backup** of the organized files into a backup folder.

Scenario: Writing a File Organization and Backup Script

Step 1: Create the Script File
Start by creating a new script file:

bash

Copy code

nano organize_and_backup.sh

Add the shebang line at the top of the file:

bash

Copy code

#!/bin/bash

Step 2: Define the Folders and Create Directories

Let's create folders to store files based on their type and a backup folder where everything will be saved.

bash

Copy code

#!/bin/bash

```
# Define the directories
TEXT_DIR="TextFiles"
IMAGE_DIR="Images"
BACKUP_DIR="backup"

# Create directories if they don't already exist
mkdir -p $TEXT_DIR
mkdir -p $IMAGE_DIR
mkdir -p $BACKUP_DIR
```

Step 3: Organize Files by Type

Now, let's add commands to move .txt files to the TextFiles directory and .jpg files to the Images directory.

bash

Copy code

```bash
#!/bin/bash

# Define the directories
TEXT_DIR="TextFiles"
IMAGE_DIR="Images"
BACKUP_DIR="backup"

# Create directories if they don't already exist
mkdir -p $TEXT_DIR
mkdir -p $IMAGE_DIR
mkdir -p $BACKUP_DIR

# Move text files and image files
mv *.txt $TEXT_DIR 2>/dev/null
mv *.jpg $IMAGE_DIR 2>/dev/null
```

The 2>/dev/null suppresses any error messages if there are no files of that type, making the script output cleaner.

Step 4: Create a Backup of the Organized Folders

Now, we'll add a command to compress the TextFiles and Images directories into a backup file stored in the backup folder. This can be done using the tar command.

bash
Copy code

```bash
#!/bin/bash

# Define the directories
TEXT_DIR="TextFiles"
IMAGE_DIR="Images"
BACKUP_DIR="backup"

# Create directories if they don't already exist
mkdir -p $TEXT_DIR
mkdir -p $IMAGE_DIR
mkdir -p $BACKUP_DIR

# Move text files and image files
mv *.txt $TEXT_DIR 2>/dev/null
mv *.jpg $IMAGE_DIR 2>/dev/null

# Create a timestamped backup of the organized files
timestamp=$(date +%Y%m%d_%H%M%S)
tar -czvf $BACKUP_DIR/backup_$timestamp.tar.gz $TEXT_DIR $IMAGE_DIR
```

This part of the script:

- Generates a timestamp with date +%Y%m%d_%H%M%S to create a unique filename for each backup.
- Uses tar with the -czvf options to create a compressed .tar.gz archive of TextFiles and Images directories, saving it in the backup folder with a unique timestamp.

Step 5: Run the Script

Make the script executable and run it to test its functionality.

bash

Copy code

```
chmod +x organize_and_backup.sh
./organize_and_backup.sh
```

Each time you run the script:

1. Any .txt files will be moved to TextFiles, and any .jpg files will be moved to Images.
2. A new compressed backup archive with a unique timestamp will be created in the backup directory.

Why This Matters

Learning to write and execute shell scripts is incredibly useful for automating repetitive tasks and managing files on Linux. Here's why shell scripting is so valuable:

- **Efficiency and Productivity**: Automating tasks saves time and reduces the need for repetitive manual commands, helping you stay focused and organized.

- **System Administration**: Many administrative tasks, such as backups, file management, and log processing, can be automated through shell scripts, making system maintenance easier and less error-prone.

- **Flexibility**: Shell scripts can be as simple or as complex as needed, making them versatile tools for tasks ranging from simple file movements to complex data processing workflows.

By practicing with shell scripts, you'll be able to tackle increasingly complex tasks on Linux, improving your productivity, optimizing system performance, and gaining control over your workflow.

CHAPTER 12: NETWORK FORENSICS

Network forensics is like detective work in the digital realm. It involves capturing and analyzing network traffic to identify malicious activity, trace attack vectors, and gather evidence for incident response and legal proceedings.

Capturing Network Traffic

To analyze network traffic, you first need to capture it. This can be done using various tools and techniques:

- **Packet sniffers:** These tools capture network traffic and store it in a file format called a packet capture (pcap) file.
  - **Tcpdump:** A command-line packet sniffer available on Linux and macOS.
  - **Wireshark:** A popular graphical packet sniffer available on Windows, Linux, and macOS.
- **Network taps:** These hardware devices are placed inline on a network segment to capture all traffic passing through it.
- **Port mirroring:** This technique allows you to configure a switch to send a copy of all traffic on a specific port to another port where a packet sniffer can capture it.

Analyzing Network Traffic with Wireshark

Wireshark is a powerful tool for analyzing network traffic. It provides a user-friendly interface for viewing and filtering captured packets, and it offers a wide range of features for analyzing protocols, identifying anomalies, and reconstructing network conversations.

- **Filtering packets:** Wireshark allows you to filter packets based on various criteria, such as IP address, port number, protocol, and content. This helps you focus on the traffic that's relevant to your investigation.
- **Analyzing protocols:** Wireshark decodes various network protocols, allowing you to see the details of each packet and understand how different protocols interact.
- **Identifying anomalies:** Wireshark can help you identify unusual traffic patterns that might indicate malicious activity, such as port scans, denial-of-service attacks, or malware infections.

Identifying Malicious Activity on the Network

Network forensics can help you identify various types of malicious activity on the network, including:

- **Malware infections:** Analyze network traffic for communication patterns associated with malware, such as command-and-control traffic or data exfiltration.

- **Intrusions:** Identify signs of unauthorized access, such as suspicious login attempts or access to sensitive data.
- **Denial-of-service attacks:** Detect unusual traffic patterns that might indicate a DDoS attack, such as a flood of requests from multiple sources.
- **Data breaches:** Analyze network traffic for signs of data exfiltration, such as large amounts of data being transferred to an external server.

Real-World Examples

- **Investigating a DDoS attack:** By analyzing network traffic during a DDoS attack, you can identify the source of the attack, the type of attack, and the targeted systems. This information can help you mitigate the attack and prevent future attacks.
- **Tracing the source of a network intrusion:** By analyzing network traffic logs and using tools like Wireshark, you can trace the path of an attacker through the network, identify compromised systems, and gather evidence for incident response and legal proceedings.

Network forensics is a critical skill for cybersecurity professionals. By capturing and analyzing network traffic, you can identify malicious activity, investigate security incidents, and protect your organization from cyber threats.Bottom of Form

CHAPTER 13: ARTIFICIAL INTELLIGENCE IN CYBERSECURITY

The future of cybersecurity is intertwined with the rise of artificial intelligence (AI). AI is revolutionizing the way we defend against cyber threats, offering powerful capabilities for threat detection, analysis, and response.

Machine Learning for Threat Detection and Response

Machine learning, a subset of AI, enables systems to learn from data and improve their performance over time without explicit programming. This is particularly valuable in cybersecurity, where threats are constantly evolving and becoming more sophisticated.

- **Anomaly Detection:** Machine learning algorithms can analyze vast amounts of data to identify patterns and anomalies that might indicate malicious activity. This can help detect previously unknown threats that might bypass traditional security rules.
- **Malware Analysis:** Machine learning can be used to analyze malware samples, classify them based on their characteristics, and identify their origins and potential impact. This can help security teams understand new malware strains and develop effective countermeasures.
- **Threat Intelligence:** Machine learning can automate the collection and analysis of threat intelligence from various

sources, such as security blogs, news sites, and vulnerability databases. This can help security teams stay informed about emerging threats and proactively defend against them.

AI-Powered Security Tools and Platforms

A growing number of security tools and platforms are leveraging AI to enhance their capabilities. These include:

- **Next-Generation Firewalls (NGFWs):** NGFWs use machine learning to identify and block malicious traffic, even if it's encrypted or uses evasive techniques.

- **Intrusion Detection and Prevention Systems (IDPS):** IDPS solutions use AI to detect and respond to suspicious activity on the network, such as port scans, denial-of-service attacks, and malware infections.

- **Endpoint Detection and Response (EDR) Tools:** EDR tools use AI to monitor endpoints (computers and mobile devices) for malicious activity, providing real-time visibility and response capabilities.

- **Security Information and Event Management (SIEM) Systems:** SIEM systems use AI to analyze security logs and alerts, identifying patterns and anomalies that might indicate a security incident.

- **User and Entity Behavior Analytics (UEBA):** UEBA tools use AI to analyze user behavior and identify anomalies that might indicate insider threats or compromised accounts.

Real-World Examples

- **Using AI to detect anomalies in network traffic:** An AI-powered network intrusion detection system can analyze network traffic patterns to identify anomalies that might indicate a cyberattack, such as a sudden increase in traffic from a specific IP address or an unusual pattern of data exfiltration.
- **Automating security incident response:** AI can automate various tasks in the incident response process, such as triaging alerts, isolating infected systems, and gathering evidence. This can help security teams respond to incidents more quickly and effectively.

Benefits of AI in Cybersecurity

- **Enhanced threat detection:** AI can detect threats that might be missed by traditional security tools.
- **Faster incident response:** AI can automate tasks in the incident response process, allowing security teams to respond more quickly.

- **Improved accuracy:** AI can reduce false positives and negatives, improving the accuracy of security alerts.
- **Increased efficiency:** AI can automate repetitive tasks, freeing up security analysts to focus on more strategic work.

- **Proactive defense:** AI can help organizations proactively defend against threats by identifying vulnerabilities and predicting attacks.

AI is transforming the field of cybersecurity, offering powerful capabilities for threat detection, analysis, and response. As AI continues to evolve, we can expect to see even more innovative applications in cybersecurity, helping organizations stay ahead of the curve in the fight against cybercrime.

CHAPTER 14: THE INTERNET OF THINGS (IoT) SECURITY

The Internet of Things (IoT) is rapidly expanding, connecting billions of devices to the internet, from smart home appliances and wearables to industrial sensors and medical devices. This interconnectedness brings tremendous benefits, but it also introduces significant security challenges.

Securing IoT Devices and Networks

Securing IoT devices and networks requires a multi-layered approach that addresses the unique characteristics of these environments:

- **Device-Level Security:**
  - **Secure Boot:** Ensure that devices boot with legitimate firmware and software.
  - **Secure Firmware Updates:** Implement secure update mechanisms to prevent unauthorized modifications.
  - **Hardware Security Modules (HSMs):** Use HSMs to securely store cryptographic keys and perform sensitive operations.
  - **Secure Communication Protocols:** Use protocols like TLS/SSL to encrypt data in transit.

- o **Access Control:** Implement strong authentication and authorization mechanisms to control access to devices.

- **Network-Level Security:**
  - o **Network Segmentation:** Isolate IoT devices from critical networks to limit the impact of a compromise.
  - o **Virtual Private Networks (VPNs):** Use VPNs to secure communication between devices and the cloud.
  - o **Intrusion Detection and Prevention Systems (IDPS):** Deploy IDPS solutions to monitor network traffic for malicious activity.

- **Cloud-Level Security:**
  - o **Secure Cloud Platforms:** Choose cloud providers that offer robust security features and comply with industry standards.
  - o **Data Encryption:** Encrypt data stored in the cloud to protect it from unauthorized access.
  - o **Access Control:** Implement strong access controls to limit who can access and manage IoT data in the cloud.

Challenges and Best Practices for IoT Security

IoT security faces several challenges:

- **Diverse Devices and Protocols:** The vast array of devices and protocols used in IoT makes it challenging to implement consistent security measures.
- **Limited Resources:** Many IoT devices have limited processing power and memory, making it difficult to implement robust security features.
- **Lack of Standardization:** The lack of standardization in IoT makes it challenging to develop and implement interoperable security solutions.
- **Legacy Devices:** Many legacy IoT devices lack basic security features, making them vulnerable to attacks.

Best Practices for IoT Security:

- **Prioritize Security from the Start:** Design security into IoT devices and networks from the beginning, rather than trying to add it as an afterthought.
- **Implement Strong Authentication and Authorization:** Use strong passwords, multi-factor authentication, and access controls to limit access to devices and data.
- **Keep Software Up to Date:** Regularly update firmware and software to patch vulnerabilities and protect against known exploits.
- **Monitor for Suspicious Activity:** Use monitoring tools and threat intelligence to detect and respond to potential security incidents.

- **Implement a Security Awareness Program:** Educate users about IoT security risks and best practices.

Real-World Examples

- **Securing Smart Home Devices:**
    - Change default passwords on smart home devices.
    - Use strong Wi-Fi encryption and a guest network for IoT devices.
    - Enable automatic security updates.
    - Monitor network traffic for suspicious activity.
- **Protecting Industrial Control Systems:**
    - Segment industrial control systems from corporate networks.
    - Implement strong access controls and authentication mechanisms.
    - Use intrusion detection and prevention systems to monitor for malicious activity.
    - Conduct regular security assessments and penetration testing.

Conclusion

IoT security is a critical concern in today's interconnected world. By understanding the challenges and best practices, organizations can secure their IoT devices and networks, protect sensitive data, and ensure the safe and reliable operation of these technologies.

CHAPTER 15: CYBER SECURITY

RETHINKING CYBERSECURITY THROUGH BLOCKCHAIN

Cybersecurity spending has increased exponentially in the past decade, with no signs of slowing. Worldwide, organizations plan to allocate more than $1 trillion between 2017 and 2021 to protect themselves from online threats, according to one industry report.[1]

Despite that staggering investment, criminal hackers are still exploiting both publicly known and unknown vulnerabilities, and intercepting device, application, and network communications. CB Insights calculated that about 6 billion confidential files were stolen between 2017 and 2018. Other industry research shows that the number and cost of cyberattacks have increased.

These sophisticated assaults often outwit traditional security methods, including authentication, key management, cryptography, and privacy challenges. With a large percentage of employees working from home due to the coronavirus pandemic, vulnerabilities are growing in new ways. So, instead of building more powerful tools, many businesses are rethinking the systems that created these vulnerabilities in the first place.

A new cybersecurity approach

Blockchain offers a different path toward greater security, one that is less traveled and not nearly as hospitable to cybercriminals. This approach reduces vulnerabilities, provides strong encryption, and more effectively verifies data ownership and integrity. It can even eliminate the need for some passwords, which are frequently described as the weakest link in cybersecurity.

The principal advantage of blockchain is its use of a distributed ledger. A dispersed public key infrastructure model reduces many risks associated with centrally stored data by eliminating the most obvious targets. Transactions are recorded across every node in the network, making it difficult for attackers to steal, compromise, or tamper with data, unless a vulnerability exists at the platform level.

Another traditional weakness is eliminated through blockchain's collaborative consensus algorithm. It can watch for malicious actions, anomalies, and false positives without the need for a central authority. One pair of eyes can be fooled, but not all of them. That strengthens authentication and secures data communications and record management.

Although blockchain contains many nontraditional features, it does take advantage of one of the most important cybersecurity tools: encryption. The distributed ledger can utilize public key infrastructure to secure communication, authenticate devices, validate configuration changes, and discover confidential devices in an **internet of things (IoT)** ecosystem. Through encryption and digital signatures, a blockchain system can shield connected thermostats, smart doorbells, security cameras, and other vulnerable edge devices. A recent Palo Alto Networks report said that 98% of IoT device traffic was unencrypted and described it as "low-hanging fruit for attackers."[2]

Also, this technology can be a weapon against distributed denial-of-service (DDoS) attacks. A blockchain-based domain name system (DNS) — the protocol for directing internet traffic — can remove the single point that allows these attacks to succeed. In 2016, a large portion of the internet went down because of a DDoS attack on the servers of one DNS host.[3]

Blockchain challenges

Organizations from multinational corporations to governments are clamoring to adopt blockchain-based cybersecurity, viewing it as the next big thing. But it's not as simple as updating an existing toolkit.

This intertwining of blockchain and cybersecurity is still an evolving approach. Not all research ideas on digital identities, decentralized storage, securing edge devices, and smart contracts align with business needs. Without careful consideration, implementation can become impractical or even impossible.

Here are some hurdles that organizations may encounter when considering blockchain as part of their cybersecurity strategy.

Data Privacy

In the public blockchain, anyone can see and retrieve data in transactions. That's a concern for businesses that want to closely control what information is publicly available.

Permissioned blockchain can help mitigate many of those privacy issues. An enterprise blockchain platform can create a permissioned network that allows only trusted parties to participate in or view transactions and to vote on decisions.

Scalability

Scalability can become a constraint when implementing blockchain, mostly due to block size and response times. In this technology, every node stores, processes, and maintains transactions in a block to ensure security and privacy. But as the number of transactions increases, small and medium-sized businesses struggle to accommodate a growing number of transactions in a block. Those increases can also slow the validation process. With limited computing and storage resources, scalability is at odds with decentralization.

Regulations

Organizations are still trying to understand how blockchain's structure and complexity fit within the evolving data privacy, compliance, and regulatory landscape. Europe's General Data Protection Regulation (GDPR) and similar laws allow individuals to demand that their data be deleted; these laws also create a "right to be forgotten" in certain cases. Since blockchain prevents parties from modifying or deleting data, the technology risks violating government rules.

Interoperability

Some blockchain platforms use a varied ecosystem for their smart contract logic, transaction schemes, and consensus models. Weak interoperability limits scalability. From the developer perspective, roadblocks can also be created from platform misconfiguration, communication mistrust, specification errors in application development, and cross-chain **smart contract** logic problems.

Thankfully, open protocols, multichain frameworks, and algorithms are taking root in blockchain and mitigating this issue. Business communications organization GS1 has published global standards for blockchain interoperability, and it is working with Microsoft and IBM on incorporating those standards into their enterprise blockchain applications. The Enterprise Ethereum Alliance is also developing business standards.

Technology risks

Blockchain offers several benefits, such as efficiency, optimization, reduced costs, and improved security. However, the technology also introduces new risks into systems when not carefully managed. These risks include:

- **Improper key management and access control.** Unlike with traditional means, end users are completely responsible for managing their digital assets. Private keys are mapped with user ownership, so unauthorized access or theft of cryptographic keys may lead to a total and irreversible loss.

- **Unintended forks and chain split attacks.** During the smart contracts upgrade process, there is a chance that some nodes may not support the changes made during the consensus phase. That can lead to a new chain splitting from the old and introduce blockchain-specific risks, such as replay, double spend, and 51% attacks. In those cases, unauthorized parties could block, reverse, or repeat transactions.

- **Inadequate encryption scheme selection and insecure operations.** Transmitting or storing sensitive data using cryptographic algorithms isn't enough to protect against man-in-the-middle attacks. A number of factors could make blockchain vulnerable to this type of intrusion, including inadequate encryption, weak or incorrect keys, key management errors, incorrect cryptographic implementation, or improper verification of digital signatures or certificates.

- **Application programming interface (API) integration.** Third parties are required for API integration, whether it's a private or public blockchain. That leads to trust issues and unintentional leakage of sensitive data.

Blockchain benefits

Even with potential barriers, the combination of blockchain and cybersecurity has intrigued executives and technology experts. In a 2019 Infosys research report, one-third of respondents cited blockchain use in developing security solutions as a top cybersecurity trend.[4] It tied for third among all topics and ranked even higher than increased demand for cybersecurity jobs.

Here are some of the factors that make blockchain promising and ways it should be managed:

- **Data protection and privacy.** The technology provides selective access to transactions and information in the distributed ledger with minimal governance. Also, blockchain doesn't give cyberattackers traditional data protection targets and the ability to undercut privacy challenges. Overall, that makes it harder to access or modify information in blockchain ecosystems.

- **Smart contract security.** Blockchain components like smart contracts, applications, APIs, digital assets, and wallets must be tested for access control, authentication, data security, and business logic validation. This provides greater confidence among participants in the permissioned chains.

- **Public key infrastructure management.** Asymmetric cryptographic keys and digital signatures are core aspects of blockchain security. In its implementation, the public key defines the digital identity to node participants. However, the private key authorizes the actions, including securely encrypting, signing, and verifying transactions. Asymmetric cryptography in blockchain provides benefits similar to those of traditional encrypted transactions.

Even with these advantages, companies should continue following security best practices, such as rate limitations, encrypting sensitive configuration files, and weeding out vulnerabilities in the development process. The authors of a related 2019 World Economic Forum paper warned about blockchain's hype and its "exaggerated security expectations."[5]

"Many have believed its cryptographic foundation to be the ultimate answer to security," according to the paper. "As a result, they have failed to implement the security controls required for trust in a blockchain to emerge." The technology is perceived as either inherently insecure or unhackable, the authors wrote, while the "truth lies somewhere in the middle."

Although usage is still limited, this intertwining of blockchain and cybersecurity isn't happening only at the fringes. It's already seen as an important tool in places where security is paramount.

The U.S. government's Defense Advanced Research Projects Agency is experimenting with the use of blockchain to create a more secure platform for transmitting messages and processing transactions. This is part of the agency's efforts to create an unhackable code for the U.S. Department of Defense (DOD). The technology immediately flags attempts to tamper with data and even provides intelligence on the attacker.

The DOD's 2019 Digital Modernization Strategy report described blockchain as a way to "not only reduce the probability of compromise, but also impose significantly greater costs on an adversary to achieve it." The U.S. military is already moving in that direction by contracting with blockchain-based data platform provider Fluree.[6]

Government officials in India announced last year that they were creating a national plan to implement blockchain for several uses, including cybersecurity. And the Saudi Arabian government and GE Ventures have invested in the startup Xage, which is using blockchain to boost cybersecurity in industrial IoT devices, according to CB Insights.

The use of blockchain to enhance cybersecurity has been gaining traction worldwide. However, the recent economic and logistics disruptions caused by the COVID-19 pandemic provide enterprises fresh incentives to find innovative solutions.[7]

Businesses now seek greater visibility and security from their networks and supply chains, even as the economy heads toward recession.[8] Digitization and resilience are imperative in a more difficult and unpredictable world. Companies want to combine security and visibility with privacy and good governance. For many companies, the answers will be found in blockchain.

CHAPTER 16: QUANTUM COMPUTING AND CYBERSECURITY

Quantum computing harnesses the mind-bending principles of quantum mechanics to perform calculations in ways that classical computers can only dream of. While this opens up incredible possibilities in various fields, it also poses a significant challenge to our current cryptographic systems.

Impact of Quantum Computing on Cryptography

Much of our current cybersecurity infrastructure relies on cryptographic algorithms that are considered secure because they are computationally difficult for classical computers to break. However, quantum computers, with their ability to leverage quantum phenomena like superposition and entanglement, can solve certain problems exponentially faster than classical computers. This has profound implications for cryptography:

- **Breaking Existing Encryption:** Quantum computers could potentially break widely used public-key cryptography algorithms like RSA and ECC, which rely on the difficulty of factoring large numbers or solving discrete logarithm problems. Shor's algorithm, a quantum algorithm, can solve these problems efficiently, rendering these encryption methods vulnerable.

- **Weakening Hash Functions:** Hash functions, used for data integrity and digital signatures, could also be weakened by quantum computers. Grover's algorithm, another quantum algorithm, can speed up the process of finding collisions in hash functions, potentially compromising their security.

Post-Quantum Cryptography (PQC)

To address the threat posed by quantum computers, the field of post-quantum cryptography (PQC) is emerging. PQC focuses on developing cryptographic algorithms that are believed to be secure against attacks from both classical and quantum computers.

Promising PQC Approaches:

- **Lattice-based cryptography:** Relies on the difficulty of solving mathematical problems involving lattices.
- **Code-based cryptography:** Uses error-correcting codes to create encryption schemes.
- **Hash-based cryptography:** Uses hash functions in new ways to create secure digital signatures.
- **Multivariate polynomial cryptography:** Relies on the difficulty of solving systems of multivariate polynomial equations.

- **Isogeny-based cryptography:** Uses the mathematics of elliptic curves in a way that is resistant to known quantum attacks.

Preparing for the Quantum Era

The transition to a post-quantum world requires proactive steps:

- **Standardization:** NIST is leading the effort to standardize PQC algorithms, evaluating and selecting promising candidates.
- **Algorithm Agility:** Designing systems that can easily switch to new cryptographic algorithms in the future.
- **Hybrid Approaches:** Combining classical and post-quantum cryptography to provide security in the transition period.
- **Key Management:** Developing robust key management systems for PQC algorithms.
- **Awareness and Education:** Raising awareness about the quantum threat and educating stakeholders about PQC.

Real-World Examples

- **Developing Quantum-Resistant Algorithms:** Researchers are actively developing and evaluating new cryptographic algorithms that are resistant to quantum attacks. For example, the CRYSTALS-Kyber algorithm is a leading candidate in the NIST PQC standardization process.

- **Exploring New Encryption Methods:** Scientists are exploring new encryption methods that leverage quantum mechanics for security, such as Quantum Key Distribution (QKD). QKD uses the principles of quantum mechanics to securely distribute encryption keys, making it theoretically impossible for eavesdroppers to intercept them.

Quantum computing presents both a challenge and an opportunity for cybersecurity. While it threatens to break existing cryptographic systems, it also drives the development of new, more secure cryptographic approaches. By actively preparing for the quantum era, we can ensure a secure digital future in the face of this technological revolution.

To dive even deeper, we could explore specific PQC algorithms in detail, analyze the mathematical foundations of their security, or discuss the challenges of implementing and deploying PQC solutions in real-world systems. We could also delve into the latest research on quantum-resistant cryptography and the ongoing efforts to standardize PQC algorithms. **1. Shor's Algorithm: A Quantum Codebreaker**

- **Factoring Large Numbers:** Shor's algorithm leverages quantum superposition and quantum Fourier transform to efficiently factor large numbers, a task that is computationally infeasible for classical computers. This directly threatens RSA encryption, which relies on the difficulty of factoring.

- **Discrete Logarithm Problem:** Shor's algorithm can also solve the discrete logarithm problem, which underpins the security of elliptic curve cryptography (ECC).

- **Implications:** The potential of Shor's algorithm to break RSA and ECC has spurred the development of post-quantum cryptography (PQC) to replace these vulnerable algorithms.

2. Grover's Algorithm: A Speed Boost for Search

- **Quadratic Speedup:** Grover's algorithm provides a quadratic speedup for searching unsorted databases. While not as dramatic as Shor's algorithm, it still impacts cryptographic hash functions.

- **Collision Resistance:** Hash functions rely on the difficulty of finding two different inputs that produce the same hash output (collision). Grover's algorithm can speed up this search, potentially weakening the collision resistance of hash functions.

- **Impact on Symmetric Cryptography:** Grover's algorithm could also affect the security of symmetric encryption algorithms like AES by effectively reducing the key space that needs to be searched. However, doubling the key length of AES (e.g., using AES-256) is generally considered sufficient to mitigate this threat.

3. Post-Quantum Cryptography (PQC): A Deeper Look

- **Lattice-based Cryptography:** This approach relies on the difficulty of solving problems related to lattices, such as finding the shortest vector in a lattice. Examples include:
  - **Learning with Errors (LWE):** A problem involving finding a hidden linear function given noisy samples.
  - **Ring-LWE:** A variant of LWE that is more efficient to implement.
  - **NTRU:** A lattice-based encryption scheme that is relatively fast and compact.
- **Code-based Cryptography:** This approach uses error-correcting codes to create encryption schemes. The McEliece cryptosystem is a classic example, based on the difficulty of decoding general linear codes.
- **Hash-based Cryptography:** This approach uses hash functions in new ways to create secure digital signatures. Examples include:
  - **XMSS:** A stateful hash-based signature scheme.
  - **SPHINCS+:** A stateless hash-based signature scheme.

- **Multivariate Polynomial Cryptography:** This approach relies on the difficulty of solving systems of multivariate polynomial equations. Rainbow is an example of a multivariate signature scheme.

- **Isogeny-based Cryptography:** This approach uses the mathematics of elliptic curves in a way that is resistant to known quantum attacks. SIDH and SIKE are examples of isogeny-based key exchange protocols.

4. Challenges of PQC Implementation

- **Performance:** Some PQC algorithms can be computationally more expensive than current cryptographic algorithms, potentially impacting performance.

- **Key Sizes:** PQC algorithms often have larger key sizes than current algorithms, which can affect storage and bandwidth requirements.

- **Integration:** Integrating PQC algorithms into existing systems can be complex and require significant modifications.

- **Standardization:** The ongoing standardization process for PQC algorithms adds uncertainty and requires flexibility in implementation.

5. Beyond Cryptography: Quantum Computing for Security

- **Quantum Key Distribution (QKD):** QKD uses the principles of quantum mechanics to securely distribute encryption keys. Any attempt to intercept the key alters its state, alerting the communicating parties.

- **Quantum Random Number Generators (QRNGs):** QRNGs generate truly random numbers based on quantum phenomena, which are crucial for cryptographic applications.

- **Quantum-Resistant Blockchain:** Researchers are exploring ways to make blockchain technology resistant to quantum attacks, ensuring the long-term security of cryptocurrencies and other blockchain-based applications.

Chapter 17: Building a Cybersecurity Career

So you're ready to embark on an exciting journey into the world of cybersecurity? Fantastic! This chapter will guide you through the essential steps to build a successful and fulfilling career in this dynamic field.

Education: Laying the Foundation

A strong educational foundation is crucial for a cybersecurity career. Here are some paths to consider:

- **Formal Degrees:**
  - **Bachelor's Degree:** A bachelor's degree in cybersecurity, computer science, information technology, or a related field provides a solid foundation in core concepts like networking, operating systems, programming, and database management.
  - **Master's Degree:** A master's degree in cybersecurity or a specialized area like digital forensics, incident response, or cryptography can provide advanced knowledge and skills.

- **Certifications:** Industry-recognized certifications validate your skills and knowledge in specific areas of cybersecurity. Some popular certifications include:
    - **CompTIA Security+:** A foundational certification that covers core security concepts.
    - **CISSP (Certified Information Systems Security Professional):** A globally recognized certification for experienced security professionals.
    - **CISM (Certified Information Security Manager):** Focuses on information security management.
    - **CEH (Certified Ethical Hacker):** Validates skills in penetration testing and ethical hacking.
    - **GIAC (Global Information Assurance Certification):** Offers a wide range of specialized certifications in areas like security administration, forensics, and incident handling.
- **Online Courses and Self-Study:** Numerous online platforms offer cybersecurity courses and resources for self-paced learning. Platforms like Coursera, edX, Cybrary, and SANS Institute provide high-quality training materials and certifications.

Skills Development: Honing Your Abilities

Beyond formal education, continuous skills development is essential in the ever-evolving cybersecurity landscape. Focus on these key areas:

- **Technical Skills:**
  - **Networking:** Deep understanding of network protocols, topologies, and security.
  - **Operating Systems:** Proficiency in Windows, Linux, and macOS, including security hardening and administration.
  - **Programming:** Knowledge of scripting languages like Python and Bash, and potentially deeper programming skills in languages like C++, Java, or Go.
  - **Cloud Security:** Familiarity with cloud platforms like AWS, Azure, and GCP, and their security features.
  - **Data Security:** Understanding of encryption, data loss prevention, and data privacy regulations.
  - **Security Tools:** Proficiency in using security tools like SIEM systems, vulnerability scanners, and penetration testing frameworks.
- **Soft Skills:**
  - **Communication:** Ability to clearly communicate technical information to both technical and non-technical audiences.

- **Problem-solving:** Analytical and critical thinking skills to identify and solve security challenges.
- **Collaboration:** Ability to work effectively in teams and with other departments.
- **Time Management:** Ability to prioritize tasks and manage time effectively in a fast-paced environment.
- **Continuous Learning:** A commitment to staying up-to-date with the latest security threats and technologies.

Job Roles in Cybersecurity

The cybersecurity field offers a wide range of career paths with varying levels of specialization:

- **Security Analyst:** Entry-level role focused on monitoring security systems, analyzing logs, and responding to security incidents.
- **Security Engineer:** Implements and manages security solutions, conducts vulnerability assessments, and develops security policies.
- **Security Architect:** Designs and implements security architectures, provides security guidance, and ensures compliance with security standards.

- **Penetration Tester:** Conducts penetration testing to identify vulnerabilities in systems and applications.
- **Security Consultant:** Provides security expertise and guidance to organizations.
- **Incident Responder:** Specializes in responding to security incidents, containing damage, and restoring normal operations.
- **Digital Forensics Analyst:** Investigates security breaches and gathers evidence for legal proceedings.
- **Malware Analyst:** Analyzes malware samples to understand their behavior and develop countermeasures.
- **Chief Information Security Officer (CISO):** Leads the organization's cybersecurity strategy and oversees all security operations.

Real-World Examples

- **CISSP Certification:** The CISSP certification is highly regarded in the industry and demonstrates a broad understanding of cybersecurity principles and best practices. It's often a requirement for senior-level security roles.
- **SANS Institute Training Courses:** The SANS Institute offers a wide range of high-quality cybersecurity training courses and certifications, covering various topics from ethical hacking to incident response. These courses are

well-respected in the industry and can help you develop specialized skills.

Building Your Career Path

- **Gain Experience:** Start with entry-level roles or internships to gain practical experience. Participate in Capture the Flag (CTF) competitions and open-source security projects to build your skills.
- **Network and Build Relationships:** Attend cybersecurity conferences and events, connect with other professionals, and join online communities.
- **Specialize:** Focus on developing expertise in a specific area of cybersecurity, such as cloud security, incident response, or digital forensics.
- **Stay Current:** Continuously learn and adapt to the ever-evolving cybersecurity landscape. Follow security blogs, read industry publications, and pursue advanced certifications.

A career in cybersecurity can be both challenging and rewarding. By building a strong educational foundation, developing essential skills, and staying current with the latest trends, you can embark on a successful and fulfilling journey in this dynamic field.

CHAPTER 18: CYBERSECURITY ETHICS AND PROFESSIONALISM

Cybersecurity professionals hold a unique position of trust. They have access to sensitive information and systems, and their actions can have a significant impact on individuals, organizations, and society as a whole. Therefore, ethical conduct and professionalism are paramount in this field.

Responsible Disclosure

When security researchers or ethical hackers discover vulnerabilities in software or systems, they have a responsibility to disclose those vulnerabilities responsibly. This typically involves:

- **Notifying the vendor or developer:** Providing the vendor with sufficient information to reproduce and fix the vulnerability.
- **Giving the vendor reasonable time to patch:** Allowing the vendor time to develop and release a patch before publicly disclosing the vulnerability.
- **Coordinating with the vendor:** Working with the vendor to ensure a coordinated disclosure that minimizes risk to users.
- **Avoiding exploitation:** Refraining from exploiting the vulnerability or sharing it with others who might exploit it.

Ethical Hacking

Ethical hacking, or penetration testing, involves using hacking techniques to identify vulnerabilities in systems and applications with the explicit permission of the owner. Ethical hackers must adhere to strict ethical guidelines:

- **Obtain written permission:** Clearly define the scope of the engagement and obtain written authorization from the system owner before conducting any testing.
- **Respect privacy and confidentiality:** Protect any sensitive information discovered during the assessment and avoid accessing data beyond the scope of the engagement.
- **Report vulnerabilities responsibly:** Follow responsible disclosure practices to ensure vulnerabilities are addressed without causing harm.
- **Act professionally and ethically:** Maintain a professional demeanor and avoid any actions that could damage the reputation of the organization or the cybersecurity profession.

Legal and Ethical Considerations

Cybersecurity professionals must be aware of and comply with relevant laws and regulations, such as:

- **Computer Fraud and Abuse Act (CFAA):** This US law prohibits unauthorized access to computer systems.

- **General Data Protection Regulation (GDPR):** This EU regulation sets strict requirements for the processing of personal data.
- **California Consumer Privacy Act (CCPA):** This California law grants consumers various rights regarding their personal information.

Beyond legal compliance, ethical considerations guide cybersecurity professionals in making responsible decisions:

- **Respect for privacy:** Protect the privacy of individuals and avoid accessing or disclosing personal information without proper authorization.
- **Avoidance of harm:** Refrain from actions that could cause harm to individuals, organizations, or systems.
- **Transparency and accountability:** Be transparent about actions and decisions, and be accountable for their consequences.
- **Professionalism and integrity:** Maintain a high level of professionalism and integrity in all interactions and activities.

Real-World Examples

- **Reporting vulnerabilities responsibly:** A security researcher discovers a vulnerability in a popular web application. They follow responsible disclosure practices by notifying the vendor, giving them time to patch, and coordinating a public announcement to minimize risk to users.

- **Adhering to codes of conduct:** A security consultant working for a company adheres to the company's code of conduct, which prohibits accessing employee data without authorization. They respect this policy even when investigating a potential security incident.

Consequences of Unethical Behavior

Unethical behavior in cybersecurity can have serious consequences:

- **Legal penalties:** Fines, imprisonment, or other legal sanctions.
- **Reputational damage:** Loss of trust, damage to professional reputation, and difficulty finding employment.
- **Harm to individuals and organizations:** Data breaches, financial losses, and disruption of services.

Ethical conduct and professionalism are essential for anyone working in cybersecurity. By understanding responsible disclosure practices, adhering to ethical hacking guidelines, and considering legal and ethical implications, cybersecurity professionals can ensure they are using their skills for good and contributing to a safer and more secure digital world.

To go even deeper, we could explore specific ethical dilemmas faced by cybersecurity professionals, discuss the role of ethics in emerging technologies like artificial intelligence, or examine case studies of ethical breaches and their consequences. **1. Ethical Dilemmas in Cybersecurity**

Cybersecurity professionals often face situations where there are no easy answers, and ethical considerations can be complex and multifaceted. Here are some examples of ethical dilemmas they might encounter:

- **Zero-day exploits:** Should a security researcher disclose a zero-day vulnerability (a previously unknown vulnerability) immediately, potentially putting users at risk, or should they wait for the vendor to develop a patch, potentially delaying protection?
- **Government surveillance:** Should a cybersecurity professional cooperate with government requests for user data, even if it means compromising user privacy?
- **Hacking back:** Is it ethical for an organization to "hack back" against an attacker, even if it means potentially violating laws or causing collateral damage?
- **Whistleblowing:** Should a cybersecurity professional report unethical or illegal activity within their organization, even if it means risking their job or facing retaliation?

These dilemmas require careful consideration of ethical principles, legal obligations, and potential consequences.

2. Ethics in Emerging Technologies

As technology advances, new ethical challenges emerge. Here are some examples related to emerging technologies:

- **Artificial Intelligence (AI):** How can we ensure that AI systems are used ethically and responsibly, especially in security applications like facial recognition and predictive policing?
- **Internet of Things (IoT):** How can we protect the privacy and security of individuals in a world where billions of devices are connected to the internet and collecting data?
- **Autonomous Systems:** Who is responsible when an autonomous system, like a self-driving car, causes harm? How can we ensure that these systems are used ethically and safely?

These emerging technologies require careful consideration of ethical implications and the development of guidelines and regulations to ensure their responsible use.

3. Case Studies of Ethical Breaches

Examining real-world cases of ethical breaches in cybersecurity can provide valuable insights and lessons learned. Here are some examples:

- **The Stuxnet Worm:** This sophisticated malware, reportedly developed by the US and Israel, targeted Iran's nuclear program. While it achieved its objective, it also raised concerns about the ethics of using cyber weapons and the potential for unintended consequences.

- **The Cambridge Analytica Scandal:** This scandal involved the unauthorized harvesting of personal data from millions of Facebook users for political advertising. It highlighted the ethical implications of data privacy and the need for greater transparency and user control over personal information.

- **The Equifax Data Breach:** This massive data breach exposed the personal information of nearly 148 million people due to inadequate security practices. It underscored the ethical responsibility of organizations to protect customer data and the consequences of failing to do so.

Analyzing these cases can help cybersecurity professionals understand the potential consequences of unethical behavior and make more informed ethical decisions.

4. Developing Ethical Guidelines and Codes of Conduct

Professional organizations like (ISC)² and ISACA have developed codes of ethics to guide cybersecurity professionals in their conduct. These codes emphasize principles like:

- **Protecting society, the common good, necessary public trust and confidence, and the infrastructure.**
- **Act honorably, honestly, justly, responsibly, and legally.**
- **Provide diligent and competent service to principals.**
- **Advance and protect the profession.**

Organizations should also develop their own codes of conduct that address specific ethical considerations relevant to their industry and operations.

5. Promoting Ethical Awareness and Education

Cybersecurity education should include a strong emphasis on ethics and professional responsibility. This can be achieved through:

- **Integrating ethics into cybersecurity curricula:** Including modules on ethics, privacy, and legal considerations in cybersecurity courses.
- **Conducting ethical hacking simulations:** Providing students with opportunities to practice ethical hacking in controlled environments.

- **Engaging in discussions and debates about ethical dilemmas:** Encouraging students to critically analyze ethical challenges and develop their own ethical reasoning skills.

- **Promoting awareness of professional codes of conduct:** Familiarizing students with the ethical guidelines and codes of conduct relevant to the cybersecurity profession.

By promoting ethical awareness and education, we can help cultivate a culture of responsibility and integrity within the cybersecurity community.

CHAPTER 19: THE IMPORTANCE OF CONTINUOUS LEARNING

In the ever-evolving landscape of cybersecurity, standing still is like moving backward. Threats are constantly emerging, technologies are rapidly advancing, and attackers are becoming more sophisticated. Continuous learning is no longer optional; it's an absolute necessity for any cybersecurity professional who wants to stay ahead of the curve.

Staying Up-to-Date with the Latest Threats and Technologies

The cybersecurity landscape is dynamic and ever-changing. New vulnerabilities are discovered, attack techniques evolve, and technologies emerge at a rapid pace. To remain effective, cybersecurity professionals must commit to continuous learning and stay abreast of these developments.

Key Areas to Focus On:

- **Emerging Threats:** Keep track of new malware strains, ransomware variants, phishing techniques, and other attack vectors. Understand how these threats work and how to defend against them.
- **Vulnerability Management:** Stay informed about newly discovered vulnerabilities in software and hardware. Learn how to assess and mitigate vulnerabilities effectively.

- **Security Technologies:** Explore new security tools and technologies, such as AI-powered security solutions, cloud security platforms, and advanced threat detection systems.
- **Compliance and Regulations:** Stay updated on changes in cybersecurity regulations and compliance requirements, such as GDPR, CCPA, and HIPAA.

Participating in Cybersecurity Communities and Events

Engaging with the cybersecurity community is an invaluable way to learn from others, share knowledge, and stay connected with the latest trends.

Ways to Participate:

- **Security Conferences:** Attend industry conferences like Black Hat, DEF CON, RSA Conference, and SANS Institute events to hear from experts, learn about cutting-edge research, and network with peers.
- **Online Communities:** Join online forums, discussion groups, and social media communities to connect with other cybersecurity professionals, ask questions, and share insights.
- **Open-Source Projects:** Contribute to open-source security projects to gain practical experience, learn from experienced developers, and give back to the community.

- **Capture the Flag (CTF) Competitions:** Participate in CTF competitions to test your skills, learn new techniques, and collaborate with others.
- **Local Meetups and Workshops:** Attend local meetups and workshops to connect with cybersecurity professionals in your area and learn about local trends and challenges.

Real-World Examples

- **Attending Security Conferences:** A security engineer attends the Black Hat conference to learn about the latest attack techniques and security vulnerabilities. They also network with other professionals and discover new security tools and solutions.
- **Following Industry Experts on Social Media:** A cybersecurity analyst follows industry experts on Twitter and LinkedIn to stay informed about emerging threats, vulnerability disclosures, and security best practices. They also engage in discussions and share their own insights.

Benefits of Continuous Learning

- **Enhanced Skills and Knowledge:** Stay current with the latest threats, technologies, and best practices.
- **Improved Job Performance:** Apply new knowledge and skills to solve security challenges and improve job performance.

- **Career Advancement:** Position yourself for career advancement by demonstrating a commitment to continuous learning and professional development.

- **Increased Earning Potential:** Acquire in-demand skills and knowledge that can lead to higher earning potential.

- **Professional Networking:** Connect with other cybersecurity professionals, build relationships, and expand your professional network.

- **Increased Job Satisfaction:** Stay engaged and motivated in your work by continuously learning and growing.

Continuous learning is essential for success in the ever-evolving field of cybersecurity. By staying up-to-date with the latest threats and technologies, participating in cybersecurity communities and events, and actively seeking out opportunities for professional development, you can ensure that your skills and knowledge remain relevant and that you are well-equipped to face the challenges of the future.

1. Advanced Threat Hunting and Intelligence

- **Threat Modeling:** Go beyond basic threat identification and delve into threat modeling methodologies like STRIDE and DREAD. Learn to proactively identify potential threats based on system design and architecture.

- **Open Source Intelligence (OSINT) Gathering:** Master advanced OSINT techniques to uncover hidden threats and actors. Explore tools and platforms like Shodan, Censys, and Maltego to gather intelligence from publicly available sources.

- **Malware Reverse Engineering:** Develop skills in reverse engineering to analyze malware samples, understand their behavior, and extract valuable threat intelligence.

- **Threat Intelligence Platforms:** Learn to utilize threat intelligence platforms like Recorded Future, ThreatConnect, and Anomali to access and analyze curated threat data.

2. Mastering Emerging Technologies

- **Cloud Security Deep Dive:** Go beyond basic cloud security concepts and delve into specific cloud security architectures, services, and best practices for major cloud providers like AWS, Azure, and GCP.

- **DevSecOps:** Embrace the DevSecOps philosophy and learn to integrate security practices throughout the software development lifecycle. Explore tools and techniques for automated security testing, continuous integration, and continuous delivery (CI/CD).

- **Artificial Intelligence (AI) and Machine Learning (ML) in Security:** Gain a deeper understanding of how AI and ML are being used in cybersecurity, including anomaly detection, malware analysis, and threat intelligence. Explore platforms and frameworks for building AI-powered security solutions.

- **Blockchain Security:** Dive into the intricacies of blockchain security, including smart contract vulnerabilities, consensus mechanisms, and cryptographic techniques. Explore tools and techniques for securing blockchain applications.

3. Specialized Learning Paths

- **Cybersecurity Specialization:** Focus on developing expertise in a specific area of cybersecurity, such as:
  - **Incident Response:** Master incident handling methodologies, digital forensics techniques, and malware analysis.
  - **Penetration Testing:** Develop advanced penetration testing skills, including exploit development, social engineering, and network pivoting.
  - **Security Auditing and Compliance:** Gain expertise in security audits, risk assessments, and compliance frameworks like ISO 27001, NIST CSF, and PCI DSS.

- o **Data Security and Privacy:** Deepen your knowledge of data encryption, data loss prevention, and privacy regulations like GDPR and CCPA.
- **Advanced Certifications:** Pursue advanced certifications to validate your expertise and demonstrate your commitment to continuous learning. Examples include:
  - o **Offensive Security Certified Professional (OSCP):** A hands-on penetration testing certification.
  - o **GIAC Certified Incident Handler (GCIH):** Focuses on incident response and handling.
  - o **Certified Cloud Security Professional (CCSP):** Demonstrates expertise in cloud security.
  - o **Certified Information Privacy Professional (CIPP):** Focuses on data privacy and protection.

4. Active Community Engagement

- **Contributing to Open Source:** Contribute to open-source security projects to gain practical experience, collaborate with other developers, and give back to the community.
- **Presenting at Conferences and Workshops:** Share your knowledge and expertise by presenting at security conferences and workshops.
- **Mentoring Others:** Mentor aspiring cybersecurity professionals and share your experience and insights.

- **Creating Content:** Write blog posts, articles, or even books to share your knowledge and contribute to the cybersecurity community.

5. Leveraging Advanced Learning Resources

- **Specialized Training Platforms:** Utilize platforms like SANS Institute, Offensive Security, and INE for in-depth training and certifications.
- **Academic Journals and Research Papers:** Stay abreast of the latest cybersecurity research by reading academic journals and research papers.
- **Security Blogs and Podcasts:** Follow security blogs and podcasts to get insights from industry experts and stay informed about emerging trends.
- **Online Learning Platforms:** Take advantage of online learning platforms like Coursera, edX, and Udemy to access a wide range of cybersecurity courses.

By actively pursuing these advanced learning strategies and resources, you can accelerate your growth as a cybersecurity professional and stay ahead in this dynamic and challenging field. Remember, continuous learning is not just about acquiring knowledge; it's about applying that knowledge to solve real-world problems and contribute to a safer digital world.

CHAPTER 20: THE FUTURE OF CYBERSECURITY

We've journeyed through the vast landscape of cybersecurity, exploring its foundations, essential skills, advanced concepts, and emerging trends. Now, as we conclude this handbook, let's recap the key takeaways and look ahead to the future of this dynamic field.

Recap of Key Concepts

- Cybersecurity Fundamentals: We started with the core principles of confidentiality, integrity, and availability, and explored the ever-evolving threat landscape, from malware and phishing to social engineering and DDoS attacks.

- Essential Skills: We delved into the technical skills needed to defend against these threats, including network security, operating system security, and the use of essential tools like SIEM systems, vulnerability scanners, and penetration testing frameworks.

- Advanced Concepts: We ventured into the frontiers of cybersecurity, exploring cloud security, data security and privacy, application security, and network forensics.

- Emerging Trends: We examined the transformative potential of AI in cybersecurity, the security challenges of the Internet of Things (IoT), the promise of blockchain technology, and the implications of quantum computing.

- Career Development: We explored the paths to building a successful cybersecurity career, from education and certifications to skills development and job roles.
- Ethics and Professionalism: We emphasized the importance of ethical conduct, responsible disclosure, and adherence to professional codes of conduct.
- Continuous Learning: We stressed the necessity of staying up-to-date with the latest threats and technologies, participating in cybersecurity communities, and actively pursuing professional development.

Advice for Aspiring Cybersecurity Analysts

- Embrace Continuous Learning: The cybersecurity landscape is constantly evolving, so commit to lifelong learning. Stay curious, explore new technologies, and never stop expanding your knowledge and skills.
- Develop a Strong Foundation: Build a solid foundation in core cybersecurity concepts, including networking, operating systems, and security principles.
- Specialize in an Area of Interest: Focus on developing expertise in a specific area of cybersecurity that aligns with your interests and career goals, such as incident response, penetration testing, or cloud security.
- Gain Practical Experience: Seek out opportunities to gain practical experience, such as internships, open-source projects, and CTF competitions.

- Network and Build Relationships: Connect with other cybersecurity professionals through conferences, online communities, and local meetups.
- Embrace Ethical Hacking: Develop ethical hacking skills to understand how attackers think and how to defend against them.
- Be a Responsible Cyber Citizen: Use your skills and knowledge to promote cybersecurity awareness and contribute to a safer digital world.

Call to Action: Contributing to a Safer Digital World

The future of cybersecurity depends on the collective efforts of individuals, organizations, and governments. We all have a role to play in creating a safer digital world.

- Individuals: Practice good cyber hygiene, stay informed about security threats, and report suspicious activity.
- Organizations: Invest in cybersecurity, implement strong security controls, and prioritize data protection and privacy.
- Governments: Develop cybersecurity policies and regulations, promote cybersecurity education and awareness, and foster collaboration between public and private sectors.

Together, we can build a more secure and resilient digital future.

The Future of Cybersecurity

The future of cybersecurity is filled with both challenges and opportunities. As technology continues to advance, we can expect to see new threats emerge and existing threats become more sophisticated. However, we can also expect to see innovative solutions and technologies that will help us defend against these threats.

The future of cybersecurity will be shaped by:

- Artificial Intelligence: AI will play an increasingly important role in threat detection, analysis, and response.
- Quantum Computing: Quantum computing will challenge existing cryptographic systems but also open up new possibilities for secure communication and data protection.
- Internet of Things: The security of IoT devices and networks will become increasingly critical as billions of devices connect to the internet.
- Blockchain Technology: Blockchain will offer new solutions for secure data storage, identity management, and supply chain security.
- Human-Machine Collaboration: The future of cybersecurity will involve a close collaboration between humans and machines, leveraging the strengths of both to create a more secure digital world.

By embracing continuous learning, ethical conduct, and a collaborative spirit, we can navigate the challenges and opportunities that lie ahead and build a safer and more secure digital future for all.

Ah, you're thinking outside the confines of the typical 20-chapter structure! I like your innovative spirit. While we've covered a lot of ground, there are always more specialized and emerging areas in cybersecurity that warrant exploration. How about we delve into a cutting-edge topic for Chapter 22?

CHAPTER 21: SECURING THE METAVERSE

The metaverse is no longer a figment of science fiction; it's rapidly becoming a part of our digital reality. As we venture into these immersive virtual worlds, the need to secure them becomes paramount. This chapter explores the intricate layers of metaverse security, examining the unique challenges, emerging threats, and cutting-edge solutions that are shaping this new frontier.

I. The Metaverse Unveiled

Before we delve into security, let's establish a clear understanding of what constitutes the metaverse. It's more than just virtual reality; it's a convergence of technologies that create interconnected, persistent digital spaces where users can interact, create, and experience a parallel reality. Key components include:

- **Virtual Reality (VR):** Immersive 3D environments experienced through head-mounted displays, offering a sense of presence and interaction.
- **Augmented Reality (AR):** Overlaying digital content onto the real world through devices like smartphones and AR glasses, blending the physical and digital realms.

- **Mixed Reality (MR):** A hybrid of VR and AR, where digital objects interact with the real world in real-time.

- **Blockchain:** Decentralized platforms and cryptocurrencies that enable digital ownership, secure transactions, and verifiable identities.

- **Artificial Intelligence (AI):** AI-powered avatars, virtual assistants, and content creation tools that enhance the metaverse experience.

- **Internet of Things (IoT):** Connected devices that gather and exchange data, creating a seamless integration between the physical and virtual worlds.

II. Unique Security Challenges in the Metaverse

The metaverse presents a new set of security challenges that differ from traditional cybersecurity domains. These challenges arise from the unique characteristics of these immersive environments:

- **Identity and Access Management:**
  - **Identity Theft and Impersonation:** Protecting digital identities and avatars from unauthorized access and manipulation is crucial to prevent identity theft, impersonation, and fraud.
  - **Authentication and Authorization:** Implementing robust authentication mechanisms, such as multi-factor authentication and biometric verification, is

essential to ensure that only authorized users can access metaverse platforms and services.

- **Decentralized Identity:** Exploring decentralized identity solutions based on blockchain technology can empower users with greater control over their digital identities and reduce reliance on centralized providers.

- **Data Privacy and Security:**
  - **Sensitive Data Collection:** Metaverse platforms collect vast amounts of user data, including personal information, biometric data, behavioral data, and interaction logs. Protecting this data from unauthorized access and misuse is paramount.

  - **Privacy-Enhancing Technologies:** Employing privacy-preserving technologies, such as differential privacy, homomorphic encryption, and federated learning, can enable data analysis and personalization while protecting user privacy.

  - **Data Breaches and Leaks:** Preventing data breaches and leaks is crucial to maintain user trust and avoid legal and reputational damage.

- **Secure Transactions and Virtual Asset Ownership:**
  - **Cryptocurrency Security:** Protecting users' cryptocurrency wallets and digital assets from theft and fraud is essential in the metaverse economy.

- **Smart Contract Vulnerabilities:** Ensuring the security of smart contracts that govern virtual asset ownership and transactions is crucial to prevent exploitation and financial losses.

- **Secure Payment Gateways:** Implementing secure payment gateways and transaction protocols is necessary to protect user financial information and prevent fraud.

- **Immersive Threats and Attacks:**

  - **Virtual World Exploits:** Vulnerabilities in metaverse platforms and applications can be exploited to gain unauthorized access, manipulate virtual environments, or disrupt services.

  - **Avatar Hijacking:** Attackers may attempt to take control of user avatars, steal virtual assets, or engage in malicious activities using compromised identities.

  - **Denial-of-Presence Attacks:** Similar to denial-of-service attacks, these attacks aim to disrupt user access to metaverse platforms or specific virtual environments.

  - **Social Engineering and Manipulation:** Attackers may leverage social engineering techniques to manipulate users within the metaverse, tricking them into revealing sensitive information or performing actions that benefit the attacker.

- **Interoperability and Standardization:**
    - o **Lack of Standards:** The absence of widely adopted standards for metaverse platforms and technologies creates challenges for interoperability and security.
    - o **Fragmentation:** The fragmentation of the metaverse across different platforms and providers makes it difficult to implement consistent security measures.
    - o **Collaboration and Standardization Efforts:** Industry collaboration and the development of open standards are essential to address interoperability and security challenges.

III. Securing the Metaverse: A Multi-Layered Approach

Securing the metaverse requires a comprehensive and multi-layered approach that addresses the unique challenges and vulnerabilities of these immersive environments. Key security measures include:

- **Strong Authentication and Authorization:**
    - o **Multi-Factor Authentication (MFA):** Implementing MFA adds an extra layer of security by requiring users to provide multiple forms of

authentication, such as a password, a one-time code, or a biometric scan.

- o **Biometric Authentication:** Utilizing biometric authentication, such as facial recognition or fingerprint scanning, can enhance security and prevent unauthorized access to user accounts and avatars.

- o **Decentralized Identity:** Exploring blockchain-based decentralized identity solutions can empower users with greater control over their digital identities and reduce reliance on centralized providers.

- **Data Encryption and Privacy-Preserving Technologies:**
    - o **End-to-End Encryption:** Encrypting data in transit between users and metaverse platforms using end-to-end encryption protects data from eavesdropping and unauthorized access.

    - o **Data at Rest Encryption:** Encrypting data stored on metaverse servers and databases protects against data breaches and unauthorized access.

    - o **Privacy-Enhancing Technologies:** Implementing privacy-preserving technologies, such as differential privacy, homomorphic encryption, and federated learning, can enable data analysis and personalization while protecting user privacy.

- **Secure Development Practices:**
    - ○ **Secure Coding Practices:** Developers should adhere to secure coding practices to minimize vulnerabilities in metaverse applications and platforms.
    - ○ **Security Testing:** Conducting thorough security testing, including vulnerability assessments and penetration testing, is crucial to identify and address security weaknesses.
    - ○ **Code Reviews and Audits:** Regular code reviews and security audits can help identify and rectify vulnerabilities before they are exploited.
- **Virtual World Security:**
    - ○ **Access Controls:** Implement access controls within virtual worlds to restrict access to certain areas, features, or content based on user roles and permissions.
    - ○ **Intrusion Detection Systems (IDS):** Deploy IDSs within virtual worlds to monitor for suspicious activity and potential attacks.
    - ○ **Anti-Cheat Mechanisms:** Implement anti-cheat mechanisms to prevent cheating and unfair gameplay in metaverse games and experiences.
    - ○ **Virtual Environment Hardening:** Secure virtual environments by applying security updates,

configuring firewalls, and disabling unnecessary services.

- **Blockchain Security:**
  - ○ **Smart Contract Audits:** Conduct thorough audits of smart contracts to identify and remediate vulnerabilities before deployment.
  - ○ **Secure Key Management:** Implement secure key management practices to protect cryptographic keys used for virtual asset ownership and transactions.
  - ○ **Blockchain Monitoring:** Monitor blockchain networks for suspicious activity and potential threats.
- **AI-Powered Security:**
  - ○ **Anomaly Detection:** Utilize AI and machine learning to detect anomalies in user behavior, network traffic, and system logs that might indicate malicious activity.
  - ○ **Threat Intelligence:** Leverage AI to gather and analyze threat intelligence from various sources, such as security blogs, news sites, and vulnerability databases.
  - ○ **Automated Security Response:** Use AI to automate security tasks, such as incident response, malware analysis, and vulnerability remediation.

IV. Real-World Examples

- **Secure Avatars:**
  - **Ready Player Me:** This platform allows users to create avatars that can be used across different metaverse platforms. They are exploring blockchain-based identity solutions to secure avatar ownership and prevent impersonation.
  - **Somnium Space:** This VR metaverse platform uses biometric authentication to verify user identities and secure avatars.

- **Virtual Asset Protection:**
  - **Decentraland:** This decentralized metaverse platform uses blockchain technology and smart contracts to secure virtual land ownership and enable secure transactions of virtual assets.
  - **The Sandbox:** This metaverse platform allows users to create and monetize their own games and experiences. They use blockchain technology to secure ownership of in-game assets and prevent fraud.

- **AI-Driven Security:**
  - **Microsoft Mesh:** This platform for collaborative mixed reality experiences is exploring the use of AI for security, including anomaly detection and threat intelligence.

- o **NVIDIA Omniverse:** This platform for 3D design collaboration is using AI to enhance security, including real-time threat detection and automated response.

V. The Future of Metaverse Security

The metaverse is still in its early stages of development, and the security landscape will continue to evolve as the technology matures. We can anticipate further advancements in the following areas:

- **Decentralized Security:**
  - o **Decentralized Identity Management:** Blockchain-based identity solutions will empower users with greater control over their digital identities and reduce reliance on centralized providers.
  - o **Decentralized Access Control:** Decentralized access control mechanisms will enable fine-grained access management and secure data sharing in the

CHAPTER 22: SECURING THE METAVERSE - ADVANCED PERSISTENT THREATS (APTS) AND THREAT HUNTING

The metaverse, with its interconnected virtual worlds and valuable digital assets, is becoming an attractive target for sophisticated attackers. This chapter delves into the realm of Advanced Persistent Threats (APTs) in the metaverse and explores advanced threat hunting techniques to proactively defend these immersive environments.

I. Advanced Persistent Threats (APTs) in the Metaverse

APTs are stealthy and continuous cyberattacks often orchestrated by well-resourced adversaries, such as nation-states or organized crime groups. They aim to establish a long-term presence within a target network to exfiltrate data, disrupt operations, or achieve other malicious goals. In the context of the metaverse, APTs pose a significant threat due to:

- **High-Value Targets:** Metaverse platforms hold valuable user data, financial information, and intellectual property, making them attractive targets for APTs.

- **Expanded Attack Surface:** The interconnected nature of the metaverse and the integration of various technologies create an expanded attack surface for APTs to exploit.
- **Novel Attack Vectors:** The metaverse introduces new attack vectors, such as avatar impersonation, virtual world manipulation, and social engineering within immersive environments.
- **Evolving Tactics, Techniques, and Procedures (TTPs):** APT groups are constantly evolving their TTPs to bypass traditional security measures and remain undetected.

II. APT Lifecycle in the Metaverse

Understanding the APT lifecycle is crucial for detecting and mitigating these sophisticated attacks. While the specific stages may vary, a typical APT lifecycle in the metaverse includes:

- **Reconnaissance:** Attackers gather information about the target metaverse platform, its users, and its infrastructure. This may involve open-source intelligence (OSINT) gathering, social engineering, and reconnaissance within virtual worlds.
- **Initial Compromise:** Attackers gain initial access to the metaverse platform, often through phishing attacks, exploiting vulnerabilities, or compromising user accounts.

- **Establishing Foothold:** Once inside, attackers establish a foothold by installing malware, creating backdoors, or compromising legitimate accounts.
- **Lateral Movement:** Attackers move laterally within the metaverse platform, exploring different virtual worlds, accessing sensitive data, and escalating privileges.
- **Data Exfiltration:** Attackers exfiltrate valuable data, such as user information, financial data, or intellectual property.
- **Maintaining Persistence:** Attackers maintain persistent access to the metaverse platform, often through backdoors, compromised accounts, or hidden infrastructure.
- **Covering Tracks:** Attackers attempt to cover their tracks by deleting logs, manipulating timestamps, or using obfuscation techniques.

III. Threat Hunting in the Metaverse

Threat hunting is a proactive approach to cybersecurity that involves actively searching for and identifying threats that may have bypassed traditional security measures. In the metaverse, threat hunting is crucial for detecting APTs and other sophisticated attacks.

- **Threat Hunting Techniques:**

- o **Hypothesis-Driven Hunting:** Develop hypotheses about potential threats and then search for evidence to support or refute those hypotheses.

- o **Indicator-Based Hunting:** Search for known indicators of compromise (IOCs), such as malicious IP addresses, domain names, or file hashes.

- o **Anomaly Detection:** Analyze user behavior, network traffic, and system logs to identify anomalies that may indicate malicious activity.

- o **Intelligence-Driven Hunting:** Leverage threat intelligence from various sources to identify potential threats and attack patterns.

- **Threat Hunting Tools and Technologies:**
  - o **Security Information and Event Management (SIEM) Systems:** Analyze security logs and events to identify suspicious patterns and anomalies.

  - o **Endpoint Detection and Response (EDR) Tools:** Monitor endpoint activity for malicious behavior and gather forensic evidence.

  - o **Network Traffic Analysis Tools:** Analyze network traffic for suspicious communication patterns and data exfiltration attempts.

  - o **Threat Intelligence Platforms:** Access and analyze curated threat intelligence data to identify potential threats and attack patterns.

- o **Data Visualization and Analytics Tools:** Visualize and analyze data to identify patterns and anomalies that may indicate malicious activity.

- **Metaverse-Specific Threat Hunting Considerations:**
  - o **Avatar Behavior Analysis:** Analyze avatar behavior, such as movement patterns, interactions, and social connections, to identify anomalies and potential threats.
  - o **Virtual World Monitoring:** Monitor virtual worlds for suspicious activities, such as unauthorized access, data exfiltration, and manipulation of virtual environments.
  - o **Blockchain Analysis:** Analyze blockchain transactions and smart contract activity to identify suspicious patterns and potential exploits.
  - o **Cross-Platform Correlation:** Correlate security events and data across different metaverse platforms to identify coordinated attacks and APT activity.

IV. Real-World Examples

- **APT Targeting Virtual Asset Exchanges:** APT groups have targeted virtual asset exchanges in the metaverse, attempting to steal cryptocurrencies and NFTs through sophisticated phishing attacks and exploits.

- **Espionage in Virtual Worlds:** Nation-state actors have been observed conducting espionage activities within virtual worlds, gathering intelligence and monitoring user interactions.
- **Data Exfiltration from Metaverse Platforms:** Attackers have exploited vulnerabilities in metaverse platforms to exfiltrate user data, including personal information and financial data.

V. The Future of APT Hunting in the Metaverse

As the metaverse continues to evolve, so too will the sophistication of APT attacks. The future of threat hunting in the metaverse will likely involve:

- **AI-Driven Threat Hunting:** Leveraging AI and machine learning to automate threat hunting tasks, analyze vast amounts of data, and identify complex attack patterns.
- **Threat Intelligence Sharing:** Increased collaboration and threat intelligence sharing between metaverse platforms and security researchers to proactively defend against APTs.
- **Decentralized Threat Intelligence:** Utilizing blockchain technology to create decentralized threat intelligence networks that are resilient to censorship and manipulation.

- **Proactive Threat Hunting:** Developing proactive threat hunting strategies that anticipate and mitigate emerging APT tactics and techniques.

Securing the metaverse from APTs requires a proactive and vigilant approach. By understanding the APT lifecycle, employing advanced threat hunting techniques, and leveraging cutting-edge tools and technologies, we can effectively defend these immersive environments and protect users from sophisticated attackers. As the metaverse continues to grow and evolve, the importance of APT hunting and proactive security measures will only become more critical in ensuring a safe and trustworthy digital future.

CHAPTER 23: OFFENSIVE AI AND THE FUTURE OF CYBER WARFARE

Artificial Intelligence (AI) is no longer just a tool for defense in cybersecurity; it's rapidly becoming a weapon in the hands of attackers. This chapter explores the emerging landscape of offensive AI, examining how AI is being used to enhance cyberattacks, the potential consequences, and the strategies for defending against this new generation of threats.

I. The Rise of Offensive AI

AI is transforming cyber warfare by enabling attackers to automate tasks, enhance decision-making, and develop more sophisticated and evasive attack techniques. Key applications of offensive AI include:

- **Automated Vulnerability Discovery:** AI algorithms can analyze vast amounts of code and identify vulnerabilities faster and more efficiently than human analysts.

- **Automated Exploit Development:** AI can be used to generate exploits that target specific vulnerabilities, potentially bypassing traditional security measures.

- **Adaptive Malware:** AI-powered malware can adapt its behavior to evade detection and maximize its impact.

- **Targeted Phishing and Social Engineering:** AI can personalize phishing emails and social engineering attacks, making them more convincing and effective.

- **AI-Driven Denial-of-Service Attacks:** AI can orchestrate and optimize DDoS attacks, making them more difficult to mitigate.

- **Automated Evasion Techniques:** AI can be used to develop evasion techniques that bypass intrusion detection systems and other security measures.

- **Autonomous Attack Systems:** AI can enable the development of autonomous attack systems that can operate without human intervention, potentially increasing the speed and scale of attacks.

II. The Potential Consequences of Offensive AI

The use of offensive AI in cyber warfare poses significant risks and challenges:

- **Increased Attack Sophistication:** AI-powered attacks can be more sophisticated, targeted, and evasive, making them more difficult to detect and defend against.

- **Accelerated Attack Speed:** AI can automate attack tasks, increasing the speed and scale of attacks, potentially overwhelming defenses.

- **Reduced Attack Costs:** AI can reduce the cost and effort required to launch cyberattacks, making them more accessible to a wider range of attackers.

- **Escalation of Cyber Conflicts:** The use of offensive AI could lead to an escalation of cyber conflicts, with potentially devastating consequences.

- **Ethical and Legal Considerations:** The development and use of offensive AI raise ethical and legal concerns, particularly regarding autonomous weapons systems and the potential for unintended consequences.

III. Defending Against Offensive AI

Defending against offensive AI requires a proactive and adaptive approach that leverages AI for defense and incorporates new security strategies.

- **AI-Powered Defenses:**

- o **AI-Driven Threat Detection:** Utilize AI to analyze network traffic, system logs, and user behavior to detect anomalies and malicious activity.
- o **AI-Powered Vulnerability Remediation:** Use AI to automate vulnerability patching and remediation.
- o **AI-Enhanced Deception Technologies:** Deploy AI-powered deception technologies to lure attackers and gather intelligence about their tactics.
- o **AI-Driven Incident Response:** Automate incident response tasks using AI to accelerate containment and recovery.

- **Adaptive Security Strategies:**
  - o **Zero Trust Security:** Adopt a zero trust security model that assumes no user or device is inherently trustworthy.
  - o **Threat Intelligence Sharing:** Share threat intelligence about offensive AI tactics and techniques to improve collective defense.
  - o **Red Teaming and Adversarial Simulations:** Conduct red teaming exercises and adversarial simulations to test defenses against AI-powered attacks.
  - o **Cybersecurity Education and Awareness:** Educate users and security professionals about the

risks of offensive AI and the strategies for defending against it.

- **International Cooperation and Regulation:**
  - **International Norms and Agreements:** Develop international norms and agreements to regulate the use of offensive AI in cyber warfare.
  - **Collaboration and Information Sharing:** Foster collaboration and information sharing between governments, organizations, and security researchers to address the challenges of offensive AI.

IV. Real-World Examples

- **Deepfakes and Disinformation:** AI-powered deepfakes are being used to create realistic but fake videos and audio recordings, potentially used for disinformation campaigns and social engineering attacks.
- **AI-Powered Spear Phishing:** Attackers are using AI to personalize spear phishing emails, making them more convincing and increasing the likelihood of success.
- **Autonomous Malware:** Researchers have demonstrated the potential for AI-powered malware to adapt its behavior and evade detection, posing a significant challenge for traditional security solutions.

V. The Future of Offensive AI and Cyber Warfare

The future of offensive AI and cyber warfare is uncertain, but it's clear that AI will play an increasingly important role in shaping the cyber threat landscape. Key trends to watch include:

- **Increased Automation and Autonomy:** Attackers will continue to automate and increase the autonomy of their attacks, potentially leading to faster and more widespread cyberattacks.
- **AI Arms Race:** A potential AI arms race between nations and organizations could lead to the development of increasingly sophisticated offensive and defensive AI capabilities.
- **Ethical and Legal Frameworks:** The development of ethical and legal frameworks will be crucial to guide the responsible development and use of offensive AI in cyber warfare.

Offensive AI is a rapidly evolving threat that poses significant challenges for cybersecurity. By understanding the potential of offensive AI, developing AI-powered defenses, and adopting adaptive security strategies, we can prepare for this new era of cyber warfare and mitigate the risks. The future of cybersecurity will depend on our ability to harness the power of AI for defense while addressing the ethical and legal implications of this transformative technology.

CHAPTER 24: THE QUANTUM REVOLUTION AND THE FUTURE OF CYBERSECURITY

Quantum computing is poised to revolutionize many fields, and cybersecurity is no exception. This chapter explores the profound implications of quantum computing for cybersecurity, examining both the challenges and opportunities that this transformative technology presents.

I. Quantum Computing Fundamentals

Before we dive into the implications for cybersecurity, let's recap the fundamental concepts of quantum computing:

- **Qubits:** Unlike classical bits, which can be either 0 or 1, qubits can exist in a superposition of both states simultaneously, allowing quantum computers to perform calculations in parallel.

- **Entanglement:** Entanglement is a quantum phenomenon where two or more qubits become linked, even when separated by vast distances. This enables quantum computers to perform certain types of calculations exponentially faster than classical computers.

- **Quantum Algorithms:** Quantum algorithms are designed to leverage the unique capabilities of quantum computers to solve specific problems, such as factoring large numbers or searching unsorted databases, much faster than classical algorithms.

II. Quantum Computing's Impact on Cybersecurity

Quantum computing has the potential to disrupt many aspects of cybersecurity, both positively and negatively:

- **Breaking Existing Cryptography:**
  - **Shor's Algorithm:** This quantum algorithm can efficiently factor large numbers and solve discrete logarithm problems, rendering widely used public-key cryptography algorithms like RSA and ECC vulnerable.

- o **Grover's Algorithm:** This quantum algorithm can speed up the search for collisions in hash functions, potentially weakening their security.

- o **Impact on Symmetric Cryptography:** While Grover's algorithm could also affect symmetric encryption, doubling the key length (e.g., using AES-256) is generally considered sufficient to mitigate this threat.

- **Enhancing Cybersecurity:**
  - o **Quantum Key Distribution (QKD):** QKD uses the principles of quantum mechanics to securely distribute encryption keys, making it theoretically impossible for eavesdroppers to intercept them.

  - o **Quantum Random Number Generators (QRNGs):** QRNGs generate truly random numbers based on quantum phenomena, which are crucial for cryptographic applications.

  - o **Quantum-Resistant Algorithms:** Researchers are actively developing new cryptographic algorithms that are believed to be resistant to attacks from both classical and quantum computers.

III. Preparing for the Post-Quantum Era

The transition to a post-quantum world requires proactive steps to ensure the continued security of our digital infrastructure:

- **Standardization:** The National Institute of Standards and Technology (NIST) is leading the effort to standardize post-quantum cryptography (PQC) algorithms, evaluating and selecting promising candidates.
- **Algorithm Agility:** Designing systems that can easily switch to new cryptographic algorithms in the future is crucial for adapting to the post-quantum era.
- **Hybrid Approaches:** Combining classical and post-quantum cryptography can provide security during the transition period.
- **Key Management:** Developing robust key management systems for PQC algorithms is essential for secure implementation.
- **Awareness and Education:** Raising awareness about the quantum threat and educating stakeholders about PQC is crucial for preparedness.

IV. Quantum Computing and Specific Cybersecurity Domains

Quantum computing will impact various cybersecurity domains in unique ways:

- **Network Security:** Quantum-resistant VPNs and secure communication protocols will be needed to protect data in transit.

- **Data Security:** Quantum-resistant encryption algorithms will be crucial for protecting data at rest and in use.
- **Cloud Security:** Cloud providers will need to adopt quantum-resistant security measures to protect user data and services.
- **IoT Security:** Securing IoT devices and networks in the post-quantum era will require lightweight and efficient quantum-resistant cryptography.
- **Blockchain Security:** Quantum-resistant blockchain technologies will be needed to ensure the long-term security of cryptocurrencies and other blockchain-based applications.
- **Artificial Intelligence:** Quantum computing could accelerate the development of AI, potentially leading to more sophisticated AI-powered attacks and defenses.

V. Real-World Examples

- **Quantum-Resistant VPNs:** Companies like Post-Quantum are developing VPN solutions that use quantum-resistant cryptography to secure network communication.
- **Quantum Key Distribution (QKD) Networks:** Several countries are investing in the development of QKD networks to secure critical infrastructure and government communication.

- **NIST Post-Quantum Cryptography Standardization:** NIST is actively evaluating and standardizing PQC algorithms to prepare for the post-quantum era.

VI. The Future of Quantum Computing and Cybersecurity

The future of quantum computing and cybersecurity is intertwined. As quantum computing technology matures, we can expect to see:

- **More Powerful Quantum Computers:** The development of more powerful quantum computers will further challenge existing cryptographic systems and accelerate the need for PQC.
- **New Quantum Algorithms:** New quantum algorithms may be discovered that have unforeseen implications for cybersecurity.
- **Hybrid Classical-Quantum Systems:** The integration of classical and quantum computing could lead to new security solutions and applications.
- **Quantum-Enhanced AI:** Quantum computing could enhance AI capabilities, leading to more sophisticated AI-powered attacks and defenses.

Quantum computing presents both challenges and opportunities for cybersecurity. While it threatens to break existing cryptographic systems, it also opens up new possibilities for secure communication and data protection. By actively preparing for the post-quantum era, embracing quantum-resistant technologies, and staying at the forefront of research and development, we can ensure a secure digital future in the face of this technological revolution.

CHAPTER 25: MASTERING SECURE CODING TECHNIQUES IN C/C++

C and C++ are powerful programming languages widely used in system programming, embedded systems, and high-performance applications. However, their low-level nature and manual memory management make them susceptible to various security vulnerabilities if not handled carefully. This chapter explores secure coding techniques in C/C++, equipping you with the knowledge and skills to write robust and secure code.

I. Understanding Common Vulnerabilities in C/C++

Before we dive into secure coding techniques, let's understand the common vulnerabilities that plague C/C++ code:

- Buffer Overflows: Writing data beyond the allocated buffer can overwrite adjacent memory regions, leading to crashes, data corruption, or even arbitrary code execution.

- Integer Overflows: Arithmetic operations that result in values exceeding the maximum or minimum representable value for an integer type can lead to unexpected behavior and vulnerabilities.

- Format String Vulnerabilities: Improper use of format string functions like printf can allow attackers to read or write to arbitrary memory locations.

- Memory Leaks: Failing to release dynamically allocated memory can lead to resource exhaustion and denial-of-service vulnerabilities.

- Use-After-Free Vulnerabilities: Accessing memory after it has been freed can lead to unpredictable behavior and potential exploits.

- Dangling Pointers: Pointers that point to invalid memory locations can lead to crashes or unpredictable behavior.

- Race Conditions: Concurrency issues where multiple threads access shared resources without proper synchronization can lead to data corruption or unpredictable behavior.

II. Secure Coding Techniques

To mitigate these vulnerabilities, developers should adopt secure coding practices throughout the software development lifecycle:

- Input Validation:

o Validate all input: Always validate user input, including data received from files, network connections, or other sources.

o Sanitize input: Sanitize input to remove or transform potentially harmful characters or sequences.

o Use safe input functions: Utilize safe input functions like fgets instead of gets to prevent buffer overflows.

- Memory Management:

o Prevent buffer overflows: Use bounds-checking functions like strncpy and snprintf to prevent buffer overflows.

o Avoid dynamic memory allocation when possible: Minimize the use of dynamic memory allocation to reduce the risk of memory leaks and use-after-free vulnerabilities.

o Use smart pointers: Utilize smart pointers like std::unique_ptr and std::shared_ptr to manage memory automatically and prevent memory leaks.

o Initialize variables: Always initialize variables to prevent unpredictable behavior and potential vulnerabilities.

- Secure String Handling:

o Use safe string functions: Utilize safe string functions like strncpy and strncat to prevent buffer overflows.

o Avoid using strcpy and strcat: These functions do not perform bounds checking and can lead to buffer overflows.

o Use string classes: Consider using string classes like std::string to manage strings safely and avoid manual memory management.

- Error Handling:

- o Handle errors gracefully: Implement robust error handling to prevent crashes and information leaks.
- o Avoid revealing sensitive information in error messages: Error messages should not disclose sensitive information that could be exploited by attackers.
- o Use exceptions: Consider using exceptions for error handling to ensure that errors are properly caught and handled.
- Concurrency and Synchronization:
- o Use thread-safe libraries and functions: Utilize thread-safe libraries and functions to avoid race conditions and data corruption.
- o Use synchronization primitives: Employ synchronization primitives like mutexes and semaphores to protect shared resources from concurrent access.
- o Avoid global variables: Minimize the use of global variables to reduce the risk of concurrency issues.
- Secure File Handling:
- o Validate file paths: Validate file paths to prevent directory traversal attacks.
- o Use secure file access functions: Utilize secure file access functions that perform bounds checking and prevent buffer overflows.
- o Close files properly: Always close files after use to prevent resource leaks.
- Other Secure Coding Practices:

o   Use static and dynamic analysis tools: Employ static and dynamic analysis tools to identify potential vulnerabilities in code.

o   Conduct code reviews: Perform code reviews to identify security issues and ensure adherence to secure coding practices.

o   Stay updated with security advisories: Keep abreast of security advisories and apply patches to address known vulnerabilities.

III. Real-World Examples

- Heartbleed Vulnerability: This vulnerability in the OpenSSL library allowed attackers to read memory from the server, potentially exposing sensitive information like passwords and private keys.

- ShellShock Vulnerability: This vulnerability in the Bash shell allowed attackers to execute arbitrary commands on the server, potentially gaining complete control of the system.

- Stagefright Vulnerability: This vulnerability in the Android media framework allowed attackers to execute arbitrary code on devices by sending a specially crafted MMS message.

IV. Advanced Secure Coding Techniques

- Address Space Layout Randomization (ASLR): This technique randomizes the memory addresses of key data areas, making it more difficult for attackers to exploit vulnerabilities.

- Data Execution Prevention (DEP): This technique prevents code from being executed in memory regions that are not designated for code execution, mitigating buffer overflow attacks.

- Control Flow Integrity (CFI): This technique enforces valid control flow paths within a program, making it more difficult for attackers to hijack control flow and execute arbitrary code.

V. The Future of Secure Coding in C/C++

As C and C++ continue to evolve, so too will the secure coding practices. Key trends to watch include:

- Language Enhancements: New language features and libraries are being developed to enhance security and reduce the risk of vulnerabilities.

- Automated Security Analysis: AI and machine learning are being used to automate security analysis and identify potential vulnerabilities in code.

- Secure Development Environments: Integrated development environments (IDEs) are incorporating security features to assist developers in writing secure code.

Conclusion

Mastering secure coding techniques in C/C++ is essential for building robust and secure applications. By understanding common vulnerabilities, adopting secure coding practices, and staying abreast of the latest security advancements, developers can create software that is resilient to attacks and protects user data and systems.

CHAPTER 26: BUILDING SECURE SMART CONTRACTS FOR THE METAVERSE

The metaverse is rapidly evolving into a vibrant ecosystem of interconnected virtual worlds, decentralized applications (dApps), and digital assets. Smart contracts, self-executing agreements written in code, play a critical role in this ecosystem, enabling automated transactions, decentralized governance, and the creation of unique digital assets. However, ensuring the security of these smart contracts is paramount to prevent vulnerabilities that could lead to financial losses, data breaches, or disruption of services.

This chapter delves into the intricacies of building secure smart contracts for the metaverse.

I. Understanding Smart Contracts in the Metaverse

Smart contracts are self-executing contracts with the terms of the agreement directly written into code. They automate the execution of agreements, eliminating the need for intermediaries and enabling trustless transactions. In the metaverse, smart contracts are used for various purposes:

- **Digital Asset Ownership:** Smart contracts can represent ownership of virtual land, digital collectibles, in-game items, and other virtual assets.
- **Decentralized Finance (DeFi):** Smart contracts power DeFi applications in the metaverse, enabling decentralized lending, borrowing, and trading of digital assets.
- **Decentralized Governance:** Smart contracts can facilitate decentralized governance in metaverse communities, allowing users to vote on proposals and manage community resources.
- **Automated Transactions:** Smart contracts can automate various transactions in the metaverse, such as buying and selling virtual assets, accessing virtual services, and participating in virtual events.

II. Security Vulnerabilities in Smart Contracts

While smart contracts offer numerous benefits, they are also susceptible to various security vulnerabilities that can be exploited by attackers:

- **Reentrancy Attacks:** These attacks exploit vulnerabilities in the contract's logic to repeatedly call a function before the previous call has completed, potentially draining funds or manipulating contract state.

- **Arithmetic Overflows and Underflows:** Arithmetic operations that result in values exceeding the maximum or minimum representable value can lead to unexpected behavior and vulnerabilities.

- **Logic Errors:** Errors in the contract's logic can lead to unintended consequences, such as incorrect execution of transactions or unauthorized access to funds.

- **Denial-of-Service (DoS) Attacks:** Attackers can exploit vulnerabilities to trigger excessive gas consumption or create conditions that prevent the contract from functioning correctly.

- **Access Control Issues:** Improper access control mechanisms can allow unauthorized users to modify contract state or access sensitive data.

- **Compiler Bugs:** Bugs in the compiler used to compile the smart contract code can introduce vulnerabilities.

- **Third-Party Library Vulnerabilities:** Vulnerabilities in third-party libraries used by the smart contract can be exploited by attackers.

III. Secure Smart Contract Development Practices

To mitigate these vulnerabilities, developers should adopt secure coding practices and follow best practices for smart contract development:

- **Formal Verification:** Use formal verification techniques to mathematically prove the correctness of the contract's logic and identify potential vulnerabilities.
- **Security Audits:** Conduct thorough security audits by experienced auditors to identify vulnerabilities and ensure adherence to best practices.
- **Code Reviews:** Perform code reviews to identify potential security issues and ensure code quality.
- **Testing and Debugging:** Thoroughly test and debug the smart contract code to identify and fix errors and vulnerabilities.
- **Use of Secure Libraries and Frameworks:** Utilize well-vetted libraries and frameworks that have been audited for security.
- **Input Validation:** Validate all input data to prevent unexpected behavior and vulnerabilities.

- **Access Control:** Implement strong access control mechanisms to restrict unauthorized access to contract functions and data.
- **Error Handling:** Implement robust error handling to prevent unexpected behavior and information leaks.
- **Gas Optimization:** Optimize gas usage to prevent denial-of-service attacks that exploit excessive gas consumption.
- **Secure Deployment:** Deploy the smart contract to a secure and reliable blockchain network.
- **Monitoring and Maintenance:** Continuously monitor the smart contract for suspicious activity and perform regular maintenance and updates.

IV. Real-World Examples

- **The DAO Hack:** This infamous hack exploited a reentrancy vulnerability in a smart contract, resulting in the theft of millions of dollars worth of cryptocurrency.
- **Parity Wallet Hack:** This hack exploited a vulnerability in a multi-signature wallet contract, allowing an attacker to drain funds from numerous user accounts.
- **The BeautyChain Hack:** This hack exploited an integer overflow vulnerability in a token contract, allowing an attacker to generate an unlimited number of tokens.

V. Advanced Secure Smart Contract Techniques

- **Formal Verification Tools:** Utilize formal verification tools like Coq and Isabelle to mathematically verify the correctness of smart contract code.

- **Symbolic Execution:** Employ symbolic execution techniques to explore all possible execution paths of a smart contract and identify potential vulnerabilities.

- **Fuzzing:** Use fuzzing techniques to generate random inputs and test the smart contract's resilience to unexpected data.

- **Upgradable Smart Contracts:** Design smart contracts with upgradeability in mind to allow for bug fixes and security updates after deployment.

- **Decentralized Security Audits:** Utilize decentralized platforms and communities for security audits and vulnerability bounties.

VI. The Future of Secure Smart Contracts

As the metaverse continues to evolve, the security of smart contracts will become even more critical. Key trends to watch include:

- **AI-Powered Security Analysis:** AI and machine learning will be increasingly used to analyze smart contract code and identify potential vulnerabilities.

- **Formal Verification as a Standard:** Formal verification may become a standard practice for high-value smart contracts to ensure their security and reliability.
- **Decentralized Security and Governance:** Decentralized platforms and communities will play a more significant role in securing smart contracts and ensuring their integrity.

Building secure smart contracts is essential for the stability and trustworthiness of the metaverse ecosystem. By understanding common vulnerabilities, adopting secure coding practices, and leveraging advanced security techniques, developers can create smart contracts that are resilient to attacks and protect user assets and data. As the metaverse continues to grow and evolve, the importance of secure smart contract development will only become more critical in ensuring a safe and thriving digital future.

CHAPTER 27: NAVIGATING THE LEGAL AND REGULATORY LANDSCAPE OF CYBERSECURITY

Cybersecurity isn't just about technical skills; it's also deeply intertwined with legal and regulatory frameworks. Understanding these frameworks is crucial for cybersecurity professionals to operate ethically, protect their organizations from legal risks, and contribute to a safer digital world. This chapter explores the complex legal and regulatory landscape of cybersecurity, providing a roadmap for navigating its intricacies.

I. Key Cybersecurity Laws and Regulations

A multitude of laws and regulations govern cybersecurity practices and data protection across different jurisdictions. Here are some of the most significant ones:

- **United States:**
    - **Computer Fraud and Abuse Act (CFAA):** This law prohibits unauthorized access to computer systems, including hacking, data breaches, and denial-of-service attacks.
    - **Digital Millennium Copyright Act (DMCA):** This law addresses copyright infringement in the digital

age, including provisions related to circumvention of digital rights management (DRM) technologies.

- o **Electronic Communications Privacy Act (ECPA):** This law protects the privacy of electronic communications, including email, phone calls, and stored data.

- o **Health Insurance Portability and Accountability Act (HIPAA):** This law sets standards for the protection of sensitive patient health information.

- o **Gramm-Leach-Bliley Act (GLBA):** This law requires financial institutions to protect the privacy of customer financial information.

- o **California Consumer Privacy Act (CCPA):** This California law grants consumers various rights regarding their personal information, including the right to know what information is collected, the right to delete their information, and the right to opt-out of the sale of their information.

- **European Union:**
  - o **General Data Protection Regulation (GDPR):** This comprehensive data protection regulation sets strict requirements for the processing of personal data of EU residents, emphasizing data protection principles like data minimization, purpose limitation, and data accuracy.

- o **Network and Information Security (NIS) Directive:** This directive requires operators of essential services and digital service providers to take appropriate security measures and notify authorities of significant security incidents.
- o **ePrivacy Directive:** This directive regulates the privacy of electronic communications, including cookies and online tracking.
- **International:**
  - o **Budapest Convention on Cybercrime:** This international treaty aims to harmonize national laws on cybercrime and facilitate international cooperation in investigating and prosecuting cybercrime offenses.

II. Legal and Ethical Considerations for Cybersecurity Professionals

Cybersecurity professionals must navigate a complex web of legal and ethical considerations in their daily work:

- **Data Protection and Privacy:** Handling personal data responsibly and complying with data protection regulations like GDPR and CCPA is crucial.
- **Incident Response and Reporting:** Responding to security incidents promptly and effectively, including

notifying relevant authorities and affected individuals, is essential.

- **Ethical Hacking and Penetration Testing:** Conducting ethical hacking and penetration testing activities within legal and ethical boundaries is crucial.
- **Vulnerability Disclosure:** Following responsible disclosure practices when discovering vulnerabilities in software or systems is important.
- **Intellectual Property:** Respecting intellectual property rights and avoiding copyright infringement is essential.
- **Law Enforcement Cooperation:** Cooperating with law enforcement investigations while protecting user privacy and organizational interests requires careful consideration.

III. Navigating the Legal Landscape: Practical Guidance

- **Understand Relevant Laws and Regulations:** Stay informed about the laws and regulations that apply to your industry and jurisdiction.
- **Develop and Implement Cybersecurity Policies:** Create and implement comprehensive cybersecurity policies that align with legal and regulatory requirements.
- **Conduct Regular Risk Assessments:** Assess and mitigate cybersecurity risks to minimize legal exposure.

- **Obtain Legal Counsel:** Consult with legal counsel on complex cybersecurity matters and ensure compliance with applicable laws.
- **Stay Updated on Legal Developments:** The legal landscape of cybersecurity is constantly evolving, so stay abreast of new laws, regulations, and court decisions.

IV. Real-World Examples

- **Data Breach Notifications:** Organizations must comply with data breach notification laws, such as GDPR and CCPA, when experiencing a data breach that compromises personal information.
- **Ethical Hacking Engagements:** Penetration testers must obtain written authorization from the target organization before conducting any security testing activities.
- **Vulnerability Disclosure Programs:** Many organizations have established vulnerability disclosure programs to encourage responsible reporting of security vulnerabilities.

V. The Future of Cybersecurity Law and Regulation

The legal and regulatory landscape of cybersecurity is constantly evolving to address new technologies and threats. Key trends to watch include:

- **Increased Regulation of Emerging Technologies:** New laws and regulations are likely to emerge to address the cybersecurity implications of emerging technologies like AI, IoT, and blockchain.

- **International Harmonization:** Efforts to harmonize cybersecurity laws and regulations across different jurisdictions will continue to promote international cooperation and information sharing.

- **Focus on Data Privacy and Security:** Data privacy and security will remain a central focus of cybersecurity law and regulation, with stricter requirements and enforcement actions.

- **Cybersecurity as a Shared Responsibility:** Laws and regulations will increasingly emphasize the shared responsibility for cybersecurity among individuals, organizations, and governments.

Navigating the legal and regulatory landscape of cybersecurity is a critical skill for cybersecurity professionals. By understanding key laws and regulations, operating ethically, and staying informed about legal developments, professionals can protect their organizations from legal risks and contribute to a safer and more secure digital world. As technology continues to advance and the cyber threat landscape evolves, the legal and regulatory frameworks will play an increasingly important role in shaping the future of cybersecurity.

CHAPTER 28: BUILDING A SECURE SOFTWARE DEVELOPMENT LIFECYCLE (SDL)

Software vulnerabilities are often the root cause of many cybersecurity incidents. To proactively address these vulnerabilities and build secure software, organizations need to integrate security into every stage of the software development lifecycle (SDL). This chapter explores the key principles and practices for building a secure SDL, ensuring that security is not an afterthought but an integral part of the development process.

I. The Secure Software Development Lifecycle (SDL)

The SDL is a comprehensive approach to software development that incorporates security considerations throughout the entire process, from initial planning to deployment and maintenance. It aims to:

- **Identify and mitigate security risks early:** By addressing security early in the development process, organizations can reduce the cost and effort of fixing vulnerabilities later.
- **Build secure software by design:** Security should be baked into the design of the software, not added as an afterthought.

- **Reduce vulnerabilities in released software:** The SDL aims to minimize the number of vulnerabilities that make it into production code.
- **Improve security awareness among developers:** The SDL promotes security awareness and education among developers, empowering them to write secure code.

II. Key Phases of a Secure SDL

A typical secure SDL consists of several key phases:

- **Planning and Requirements:**
  - **Security Requirements Gathering:** Identify and document security requirements early in the planning phase.
  - **Risk Assessment:** Conduct a risk assessment to identify potential security threats and vulnerabilities.
  - **Security Design:** Incorporate security considerations into the design of the software architecture and components.
- **Implementation:**
  - **Secure Coding Practices:** Adhere to secure coding standards and best practices to minimize vulnerabilities in code.

- o **Code Reviews and Static Analysis:** Conduct code reviews and use static analysis tools to identify potential security issues.
- o **Use of Secure Libraries and Frameworks:** Utilize well-vetted libraries and frameworks that have been audited for security.

- **Testing:**
  - o **Dynamic Analysis:** Perform dynamic analysis, such as penetration testing and fuzzing, to identify vulnerabilities in the running application.
  - o **Security Testing:** Conduct specific security tests, such as authentication testing, authorization testing, and input validation testing.
  - o **Vulnerability Scanning:** Use vulnerability scanners to identify known vulnerabilities in the application and its dependencies.

- **Deployment:**
  - o **Secure Deployment Practices:** Follow secure deployment practices to ensure the application is deployed in a secure environment.
  - o **Configuration Management:** Securely configure the application and its environment to minimize security risks.

- o **Vulnerability Remediation:** Address any identified vulnerabilities before deploying the application to production.
- **Maintenance:**
  - o **Security Monitoring:** Monitor the application for suspicious activity and security incidents.
  - o **Incident Response:** Establish an incident response plan to address security breaches and other incidents.
  - o **Patching and Updates:** Regularly apply security patches and updates to address newly discovered vulnerabilities.

III. Integrating Security into the Development Process

Integrating security into the SDL requires a cultural shift and a commitment from all stakeholders:

- **Security Champions:** Identify security champions within the development team to promote security awareness and best practices.
- **Training and Education:** Provide developers with training on secure coding practices, security testing, and vulnerability remediation.

- **Security Tools and Automation:** Integrate security tools and automation into the development process to streamline security testing and analysis.
- **Collaboration and Communication:** Foster collaboration and communication between developers, security teams, and operations teams to ensure that security is addressed throughout the SDL.

IV. Real-World Examples

- **Microsoft Security Development Lifecycle (SDL):** Microsoft has a mature SDL that has significantly improved the security of its software products.
- **OWASP Secure Software Development Lifecycle Project:** The Open Web Application Security Project (OWASP) provides resources and guidance for building a secure SDL.
- **ISO/IEC 27034-1:2011:** This international standard provides guidance on information security in the software development lifecycle.

V. Advanced SDL Concepts

- **Threat Modeling:** Use threat modeling methodologies like STRIDE and DREAD to proactively identify and mitigate potential threats.

- **Security Requirements Engineering:** Develop comprehensive security requirements and integrate them into the software development process.

- **Secure Design Patterns:** Utilize secure design patterns to address common security challenges in software architecture.

- **Static Application Security Testing (SAST):** Employ SAST tools to analyze source code for potential vulnerabilities.

- **Dynamic Application Security Testing (DAST):** Use DAST tools to test the running application for vulnerabilities.

- **Interactive Application Security Testing (IAST):** Combine SAST and DAST techniques to provide more comprehensive security testing.

VI. The Future of the Secure SDL

As software development practices evolve, so too will the secure SDL. Key trends to watch include:

- **DevSecOps:** Integrating security into DevOps practices to enable continuous security throughout the software development lifecycle.

- **AI-Powered Security:** Leveraging AI and machine learning to automate security testing, analysis, and remediation.
- **Shift-Left Security:** Moving security testing and analysis earlier in the development process to identify and address vulnerabilities sooner.

Building a secure SDL is essential for creating secure software and protecting organizations from cyber threats. By integrating security into every stage of the development process, promoting security awareness among developers, and leveraging advanced security techniques, organizations can create software that is resilient to attacks and protects user data and systems.

CHAPTER 29: CYBERSECURITY IN THE AGE OF DISRUPTIVE TECHNOLOGIES

The digital world is in constant flux, with disruptive technologies emerging at an unprecedented pace. These technologies, while offering immense potential for innovation and progress, also introduce new cybersecurity challenges and reshape the threat landscape. This chapter explores the cybersecurity implications of several disruptive technologies, equipping you with the knowledge and foresight to navigate the future of cybersecurity.

I. Artificial Intelligence (AI) and Machine Learning (ML)

AI and ML are transforming various aspects of cybersecurity, both for defenders and attackers:

- **AI-Powered Cybersecurity Solutions:**

- o **Threat Detection and Response:** AI algorithms can analyze vast amounts of data to detect anomalies, identify malicious patterns, and automate incident response.

- o **Vulnerability Management:** AI can assist in identifying and prioritizing vulnerabilities, automating patching, and predicting future threats.

- o **Security Automation:** AI can automate various security tasks, such as malware analysis, phishing detection, and user behavior analysis.

- **AI-Enabled Cyberattacks:**

  - o **Adaptive Malware:** AI-powered malware can adapt its behavior to evade detection and maximize its impact.

  - o **Automated Exploit Development:** AI can be used to generate exploits that target specific vulnerabilities.

  - o **Targeted Phishing and Social Engineering:** AI can personalize phishing emails and social engineering attacks, making them more convincing.

- **Challenges and Considerations:**

  - o **Adversarial AI:** Attackers can use AI to evade AI-powered defenses, requiring the development of robust and resilient AI models.

- **Bias and Fairness:** AI models can inherit biases from training data, leading to unfair or discriminatory outcomes.
- **Explainability and Transparency:** Understanding how AI models make decisions is crucial for building trust and ensuring accountability.

II. Internet of Things (IoT) and Edge Computing

The proliferation of IoT devices and the rise of edge computing present unique cybersecurity challenges:

- **Increased Attack Surface:** Billions of connected devices expand the attack surface, creating more entry points for attackers.
- **Device Heterogeneity:** The diversity of IoT devices and protocols makes it challenging to implement consistent security measures.
- **Resource Constraints:** Many IoT devices have limited processing power and memory, making it difficult to implement robust security features.
- **Data Privacy and Security:** Protecting sensitive data collected and processed by IoT devices is crucial.
- **Security Strategies:**
  - **Secure Device Design:** Incorporate security into the design of IoT devices from the outset.

- o **Secure Communication:** Use secure protocols and encryption to protect data in transit.
- o **Device Authentication and Authorization:** Implement strong authentication and authorization mechanisms to control access to devices.
- o **Firmware Updates and Patching:** Regularly update firmware and apply security patches to address vulnerabilities.
- o **Edge Security:** Secure edge computing environments to protect data processed and stored at the edge.

III. Blockchain and Decentralized Technologies

Blockchain and decentralized technologies offer both opportunities and challenges for cybersecurity:

- **Enhanced Security:**
  - o **Decentralized Identity:** Blockchain can enable self-sovereign identity, giving users more control over their digital identities.
  - o **Secure Data Storage:** Blockchain can provide secure and tamper-proof data storage.
  - o **Secure Transactions:** Blockchain can facilitate secure and transparent transactions.
- **New Attack Vectors:**

- o **Smart Contract Vulnerabilities:** Exploiting vulnerabilities in smart contracts can lead to financial losses or data breaches.
- o **51% Attacks:** In some blockchain networks, attackers with sufficient computing power can manipulate transactions or double-spend coins.
- o **Cryptocurrency Theft:** Attackers can target cryptocurrency wallets and exchanges to steal digital assets.

- **Security Considerations:**
  - o **Secure Smart Contract Development:** Adopt secure coding practices and conduct thorough audits to ensure the security of smart contracts.
  - o **Blockchain Security Best Practices:** Follow best practices for securing blockchain networks and transactions.
  - o **Cryptocurrency Wallet Security:** Use secure wallets and implement strong security measures to protect digital assets.

IV. Quantum Computing

Quantum computing has the potential to revolutionize cybersecurity, but it also poses significant threats:

- **Breaking Existing Cryptography:** Quantum computers could break widely used public-key cryptography algorithms, requiring the adoption of post-quantum cryptography (PQC).
- **Enhancing Cybersecurity:** Quantum technologies like QKD and QRNGs can enhance security and protect against quantum attacks.
- **Preparing for the Quantum Era:**
  - **Standardize PQC Algorithms:** Adopt and implement standardized PQC algorithms.
  - **Develop Quantum-Resistant Infrastructure:** Transition to quantum-resistant infrastructure and systems.
  - **Research and Development:** Invest in research and development of quantum-resistant technologies and solutions.

V. Extended Reality (XR) and the Metaverse

XR technologies, including virtual reality (VR), augmented reality (AR), and mixed reality (MR), are creating immersive digital environments with unique cybersecurity challenges:

- **Securing Digital Identities:** Protecting user identities and avatars from theft, impersonation, and manipulation.

- **Data Privacy and Security:** Safeguarding user data, including personal information, biometric data, and behavioral data, in immersive environments.
- **Secure Transactions:** Ensuring the security of digital transactions and virtual asset ownership in the metaverse economy.
- **Immersive Threats:** Addressing new forms of attacks, such as virtual world exploits, avatar hijacking, and denial-of-presence attacks.
- **Security Strategies:**
  - **Strong Authentication and Authorization:** Implement robust authentication mechanisms and access controls.
  - **Data Encryption and Privacy-Preserving Technologies:** Employ encryption and privacy-enhancing technologies to protect user data.
  - **Secure Development Practices:** Develop secure XR applications and platforms using secure coding practices and security testing.
  - **Virtual World Security:** Implement security measures within virtual worlds, such as access controls and intrusion detection systems.

VI. Biometric Authentication and Security

Biometric authentication is becoming increasingly prevalent, but it also introduces new security and privacy considerations:

- **Spoofing and Replay Attacks:** Attackers may attempt to spoof biometric systems using fake fingerprints, masks, or recorded voice samples.
- **Data Breaches and Template Theft:** Biometric templates stored in databases can be stolen in data breaches, leading to identity theft and fraud.
- **Privacy Concerns:** The collection and use of biometric data raise privacy concerns, particularly regarding surveillance and tracking.
- **Security Measures:**
    - **Liveness Detection:** Implement liveness detection mechanisms to prevent spoofing attacks.
    - **Template Protection:** Securely store and protect biometric templates using encryption and access controls.
    - **Privacy-Preserving Biometrics:** Explore privacy-preserving biometric techniques, such as homomorphic encryption and secure multi-party computation.

VII. The Future of Cybersecurity in a Disruptive World

The future of cybersecurity will be shaped by the ongoing evolution of disruptive technologies. To stay ahead of the curve, cybersecurity professionals need to:

- **Embrace Continuous Learning:** Continuously learn about new technologies, threats, and security strategies.
- **Adapt to Change:** Be prepared to adapt to the changing threat landscape and embrace new security paradigms.
- **Collaborate and Share Information:** Foster collaboration and information sharing between individuals, organizations, and governments to address cybersecurity challenges collectively.
- **Promote Ethical and Responsible Technology Use:** Advocate for the ethical and responsible use of technology to ensure a safe and secure digital future.

Disruptive technologies are reshaping the cybersecurity landscape, presenting both challenges and opportunities. By understanding the implications of these technologies, adopting proactive security measures, and fostering a culture of continuous learning and collaboration, we can navigate the complexities of the future and build a more secure and resilient digital world

CHAPTER 30: CYBERSECURITY FOR CRITICAL INFRASTRUCTURE

Critical infrastructure encompasses the essential systems and assets that are vital to a nation's functioning, including sectors like energy, healthcare, transportation, finance, and government. Protecting these systems from cyberattacks is paramount to national security, economic stability, and public safety. This chapter delves into the specialized domain of cybersecurity for critical infrastructure, exploring the unique challenges, advanced threats, and robust security strategies required to safeguard these vital assets.

I. Understanding Critical Infrastructure

Critical infrastructure sectors are interconnected and interdependent, making them vulnerable to cascading failures if one sector is compromised. Key sectors include:

- **Energy:** Power generation, transmission, and distribution systems.

- **Healthcare:** Hospitals, clinics, medical devices, and healthcare information systems.
- **Transportation:** Road, rail, air, and maritime transportation systems.
- **Finance:** Banks, financial institutions, and payment systems.
- **Government:** Government agencies and critical information systems.
- **Water and Wastewater:** Water treatment and distribution systems.
- **Communications:** Telecommunications networks and infrastructure.

II. Unique Cybersecurity Challenges for Critical Infrastructure

Securing critical infrastructure presents unique challenges compared to other sectors:

- **Legacy Systems:** Many critical infrastructure systems rely on legacy technologies that may be outdated and vulnerable to cyberattacks.
- **Industrial Control Systems (ICS):** ICS, used to control physical processes in critical infrastructure, often have specialized security requirements and may be susceptible to attacks that disrupt operations or cause physical damage.

- **Interconnectedness and Interdependencies:** The interconnected nature of critical infrastructure sectors creates the risk of cascading failures if one sector is compromised.

- **Nation-State Threats:** Critical infrastructure is often targeted by nation-state actors seeking to disrupt essential services, steal sensitive data, or gain a strategic advantage.

- **Insider Threats:** Employees or contractors with access to critical systems can pose a significant insider threat.

- **Physical Security:** Physical security breaches can also compromise cybersecurity, highlighting the need for a holistic security approach.

III. Advanced Threats to Critical Infrastructure

Critical infrastructure faces a range of sophisticated cyber threats:

- **Advanced Persistent Threats (APTs):** Well-resourced attackers, often nation-state sponsored, can launch APTs to gain long-term access to critical systems, steal data, or disrupt operations.

- **Targeted Attacks:** Attackers may launch targeted attacks against specific critical infrastructure organizations or systems, using tailored malware and exploit techniques.

- **Supply Chain Attacks:** Compromising the supply chain of critical infrastructure components can provide attackers with access to sensitive systems or introduce vulnerabilities.

- **Ransomware Attacks:** Ransomware attacks can disrupt critical services and cause significant financial losses, as seen in the Colonial Pipeline attack.
- **Disinformation and Propaganda:** Attackers may spread disinformation and propaganda to undermine public trust in critical infrastructure or create social unrest.

IV. Securing Critical Infrastructure: A Multi-Layered Approach

Protecting critical infrastructure requires a multi-layered and comprehensive cybersecurity strategy:

- **Risk Management and Assessment:** Conduct thorough risk assessments to identify vulnerabilities and prioritize security measures.
- **Security Governance and Compliance:** Establish strong security governance frameworks and comply with relevant regulations and standards, such as the NIST Cybersecurity Framework.
- **Network Security:** Implement robust network security measures, including firewalls, intrusion detection systems, and secure network segmentation.

- **Endpoint Security:** Secure endpoints, such as workstations, servers, and ICS devices, with strong authentication, access controls, and endpoint detection and response (EDR) solutions.

- **Data Security:** Protect sensitive data with encryption, access controls, and data loss prevention (DLP) solutions.

- **Vulnerability Management:** Implement a robust vulnerability management program to identify and remediate vulnerabilities in a timely manner.

- **Incident Response:** Develop and exercise incident response plans to effectively handle security incidents and minimize downtime.

- **Supply Chain Security:** Secure the supply chain of critical infrastructure components by vetting suppliers, conducting security assessments, and implementing secure procurement practices.

- **Workforce Training and Awareness:** Train employees on cybersecurity best practices and raise awareness about potential threats.

- **Collaboration and Information Sharing:** Foster collaboration and information sharing between critical infrastructure organizations, government agencies, and security researchers to enhance collective defense.

V. Real-World Examples

- **Stuxnet Attack:** This sophisticated malware, reportedly developed by the US and Israel, targeted Iran's nuclear program, demonstrating the potential for cyberattacks to disrupt critical infrastructure.

- **Ukraine Power Grid Attacks:** Cyberattacks on Ukraine's power grid in 2015 and 2016 caused widespread power outages, highlighting the vulnerability of critical infrastructure to disruption.

- **NotPetya Attack:** This global cyberattack in 2017 caused billions of dollars in damages by disrupting operations in various sectors, including transportation, healthcare, and finance.

VI. The Future of Cybersecurity for Critical Infrastructure

The future of cybersecurity for critical infrastructure will be shaped by:

- **Emerging Technologies:** The adoption of new technologies, such as AI, IoT, and 5G, will introduce new security challenges and require innovative security solutions.

- **Increased Interconnectivity:** The increasing interconnectivity of critical infrastructure systems will amplify the risk of cascading failures and require stronger collaboration and information sharing.

- **Nation-State Threats:** The threat from nation-state actors will continue to evolve, requiring advanced threat detection and mitigation capabilities.
- **Resilience and Recovery:** Building resilience and ensuring rapid recovery from cyberattacks will be crucial for maintaining essential services.

Protecting critical infrastructure from cyber threats is a national priority. By understanding the unique challenges, adopting a multi-layered security approach, and staying ahead of emerging threats, we can safeguard these vital assets and ensure the continued functioning of our societies and economies.

CHAPTER 31: CYBERSECURITY FOR INDUSTRIAL CONTROL SYSTEMS (ICS)

Industrial Control Systems (ICS) form the backbone of critical infrastructure, controlling essential processes in sectors like energy, manufacturing, transportation, and healthcare. These systems, often relying on specialized hardware and software, face unique cybersecurity challenges due to their operational technology (OT) environments and the potential for physical consequences in the event of a cyberattack. This chapter delves into the specialized domain of ICS cybersecurity, exploring the threats, vulnerabilities, and security measures required to protect these vital systems.

I. Understanding Industrial Control Systems (ICS)

ICS are computerized systems used to monitor and control physical processes in industrial environments. They encompass a range of components, including:

- **Supervisory Control and Data Acquisition (SCADA) Systems:** These systems provide centralized monitoring and control of geographically dispersed assets and processes.
- **Distributed Control Systems (DCS):** These systems control localized processes within a facility, often using interconnected controllers and sensors.
- **Programmable Logic Controllers (PLCs):** These digital computers control manufacturing processes, such as assembly lines and robotic systems.
- **Remote Terminal Units (RTUs):** These devices collect data from sensors and transmit it to SCADA systems or other control centers.
- **Human-Machine Interfaces (HMIs):** These interfaces allow operators to monitor and control industrial processes.

II. Unique Cybersecurity Challenges for ICS

Securing ICS presents unique challenges compared to traditional IT systems:

- **Legacy Systems:** Many ICS rely on legacy technologies that may be outdated, unsupported, and vulnerable to cyberattacks.

- **Convergence of IT and OT:** The increasing convergence of IT and OT networks creates new attack vectors and blurs traditional security boundaries.

- **Real-Time Requirements:** ICS often have strict real-time requirements, making it challenging to implement security measures that could introduce latency or disrupt operations.

- **Safety and Availability:** Cyberattacks on ICS can have safety and availability implications, potentially causing physical damage, disrupting essential services, or even endangering human lives.

- **Specialized Protocols and Technologies:** ICS often use specialized protocols and technologies that may not be well-understood by traditional cybersecurity professionals.

- **Limited Visibility and Control:** Organizations may have limited visibility and control over their ICS environments, especially in cases where third-party vendors manage or maintain the systems.

III. Threats to Industrial Control Systems

ICS face a range of cyber threats, including:

- **Targeted Attacks:** Attackers may launch targeted attacks against specific ICS, using tailored malware and exploit techniques to disrupt operations or cause physical damage.
- **Advanced Persistent Threats (APTs):** Well-resourced attackers can launch APTs to gain long-term access to ICS, steal sensitive data, or sabotage operations.
- **Ransomware Attacks:** Ransomware attacks can disrupt ICS operations and cause significant financial losses, as seen in attacks on manufacturing facilities and pipeline operators.
- **Supply Chain Attacks:** Compromising the supply chain of ICS components can provide attackers with access to sensitive systems or introduce vulnerabilities.
- **Insider Threats:** Employees or contractors with access to ICS can pose a significant insider threat, either intentionally or unintentionally.
- **Physical Attacks:** Physical attacks on ICS facilities or devices can also compromise cybersecurity.

IV. Securing Industrial Control Systems

Protecting ICS requires a comprehensive and multi-layered cybersecurity strategy:

- **Risk Management and Assessment:** Conduct thorough risk assessments to identify vulnerabilities and prioritize security measures.

- **Security Governance and Compliance:** Establish strong security governance frameworks and comply with relevant regulations and standards, such as the NIST Cybersecurity Framework and the ISA/IEC 62443 series of standards.

- **Network Security:** Implement robust network security measures, including firewalls, intrusion detection systems, and secure network segmentation to isolate ICS networks from IT networks.

- **Endpoint Security:** Secure endpoints, such as PLCs, RTUs, and HMIs, with strong authentication, access controls, and security hardening.

- **Vulnerability Management:** Implement a robust vulnerability management program to identify and remediate vulnerabilities in a timely manner, considering the operational constraints of ICS environments.

- **Incident Response:** Develop and exercise incident response plans to effectively handle security incidents and minimize downtime, focusing on the unique recovery needs of ICS.

- **Supply Chain Security:** Secure the supply chain of ICS components by vetting suppliers, conducting security assessments, and implementing secure procurement practices.

- **Workforce Training and Awareness:** Train employees on ICS cybersecurity best practices and raise awareness about potential threats.

- **Physical Security:** Integrate physical security measures to protect ICS facilities and devices from unauthorized access and tampering.

- **Collaboration and Information Sharing:** Foster collaboration and information sharing between ICS operators, vendors, government agencies, and security researchers to enhance collective defense.

V. Real-World Examples

- **Stuxnet Attack:** This sophisticated malware targeted Iran's nuclear program, demonstrating the potential for cyberattacks to disrupt critical infrastructure and cause physical damage.

- **Ukraine Power Grid Attacks:** Cyberattacks on Ukraine's power grid caused widespread power outages, highlighting the vulnerability of ICS to disruption.

- **Triton Attack:** This malware targeted a safety instrumented system (SIS) at a petrochemical facility, demonstrating the potential for cyberattacks to cause safety incidents.

VI. The Future of ICS Cybersecurity

The future of ICS cybersecurity will be shaped by:

- **Emerging Technologies:** The adoption of new technologies, such as AI, IoT, and 5G, in ICS environments will introduce new security challenges and require innovative security solutions.
- **Increased Connectivity:** The increasing connectivity of ICS to IT networks and the internet will expand the attack surface and require stronger security measures.
- **Sophisticated Threats:** Attackers will continue to develop more sophisticated malware and exploit techniques targeting ICS.
- **Resilience and Recovery:** Building resilience and ensuring rapid recovery from cyberattacks will be crucial for maintaining the operational continuity of critical infrastructure.

Protecting ICS from cyber threats is essential for the safe and reliable operation of critical infrastructure. By understanding the unique challenges, adopting a comprehensive security strategy, and staying ahead of emerging threats, we can safeguard these vital systems and ensure the continued functioning of our societies and economies.

CHAPTER 32: CYBERSECURITY FOR SPACE SYSTEMS

As humanity expands its reach into space, cybersecurity becomes increasingly critical for protecting the satellites, spacecraft, and ground infrastructure that enable space exploration, communication, and scientific discovery. This chapter explores the unique challenges and security considerations for safeguarding space systems from cyber threats.

I. Understanding Space Systems

Space systems encompass a wide range of technologies and infrastructure, including:

- **Satellites:** These orbiting devices provide various services, including communication, navigation, Earth observation, and scientific research.
- **Spacecraft:** These vehicles, including rockets, capsules, and probes, are used for space exploration and transportation.
- **Ground Stations:** These facilities communicate with and control space assets, receiving and transmitting data.
- **Space-Based Networks:** These networks connect satellites and ground stations, enabling communication and data exchange.

II. Unique Cybersecurity Challenges for Space Systems

Securing space systems presents unique challenges compared to terrestrial systems:

- **Remote and Hostile Environment:** Space systems operate in a remote and hostile environment, making physical access for maintenance and repairs difficult.
- **Limited Bandwidth and Latency:** Communication with space assets can be limited by bandwidth and latency, making real-time monitoring and response challenging.
- **Radiation and Environmental Factors:** Space radiation and other environmental factors can affect the performance

and reliability of electronic components, potentially creating vulnerabilities.

- **Supply Chain Complexity:** The supply chain for space systems is often complex and global, increasing the risk of counterfeit components or malicious tampering.
- **Nation-State Threats:** Space systems are often targeted by nation-state actors seeking to disrupt critical services, steal sensitive data, or gain a strategic advantage.
- **Emerging Technologies:** The integration of new technologies, such as AI and IoT, into space systems introduces new security challenges.

III. Threats to Space Systems

Space systems face a range of cyber threats, including:

- **Jamming and Interference:** Attackers can jam or interfere with satellite communication signals, disrupting services or denying access to critical data.
- **Spoofing and Deception:** Attackers can spoof satellite signals or inject false data, potentially misleading navigation systems or compromising Earth observation data.
- **Command and Control Takeover:** Attackers can attempt to gain control of satellites or spacecraft, potentially

altering their orbits, disrupting their functions, or even destroying them.

- **Data Breaches and Espionage:** Attackers can target ground stations or space-based networks to steal sensitive data or intellectual property.
- **Denial-of-Service Attacks:** Attackers can launch denial-of-service attacks against ground stations or satellite communication links to disrupt services.
- **Supply Chain Attacks:** Compromising the supply chain of space system components can provide attackers with access to sensitive systems or introduce vulnerabilities.

IV. Securing Space Systems

Protecting space systems requires a comprehensive and multi-layered cybersecurity strategy:

- **Secure Design and Development:** Incorporate security into the design and development of space systems from the outset, considering the unique challenges of the space environment.
- **Secure Communication:** Implement secure communication protocols and encryption to protect data transmitted between space assets and ground stations.
- **Satellite Hardening:** Harden satellites and spacecraft against cyberattacks by implementing security measures

such as secure boot, access controls, and intrusion detection systems.

- **Ground Station Security:** Secure ground stations with robust network security measures, access controls, and physical security.

- **Supply Chain Security:** Secure the supply chain of space system components by vetting suppliers, conducting security assessments, and implementing secure procurement practices.

- **Threat Intelligence and Monitoring:** Monitor for potential threats and vulnerabilities, leveraging threat intelligence and advanced analytics to detect and respond to attacks.

- **Incident Response:** Develop and exercise incident response plans to effectively handle security incidents and minimize downtime.

- **International Collaboration:** Foster international collaboration and information sharing to address the global nature of space cybersecurity threats.

V. Real-World Examples

- **GPS Spoofing:** Attackers have spoofed GPS signals to mislead ships and aircraft, highlighting the vulnerability of navigation systems to cyberattacks.

- **Satellite Jamming:** Nation-state actors have jammed satellite communication signals to disrupt military operations and civilian services.
- **Data Breaches at Space Agencies:** Space agencies have experienced data breaches, highlighting the need for strong cybersecurity measures to protect sensitive information.

VI. The Future of Space Cybersecurity

The future of space cybersecurity will be shaped by:

- **Increased Space Activity:** The growing number of satellites and space missions will expand the attack surface and require more sophisticated security measures.
- **Emerging Technologies:** The integration of new technologies, such as AI, IoT, and quantum computing, into space systems will introduce new security challenges and opportunities.
- **Space-Based Cybersecurity Infrastructure:** The development of dedicated cybersecurity infrastructure in space, such as secure communication networks and threat detection systems, will be crucial for protecting space assets.
- **International Cooperation:** International cooperation and the development of norms and standards for responsible

behavior in space will be essential for ensuring the long-term security and sustainability of space activities.

Protecting space systems from cyber threats is crucial for maintaining essential services, supporting scientific discovery, and ensuring national security. By understanding the unique challenges, adopting a comprehensive security strategy, and staying ahead of emerging threats, we can safeguard these vital assets and enable the continued exploration and utilization of space.

CHAPTER 33: CYBERSECURITY IN THE AGE OF QUANTUM COMPUTING

Quantum computing is no longer a futuristic concept; it's rapidly approaching reality, with profound implications for cybersecurity. This chapter delves into the transformative potential of quantum computing, exploring how it will revolutionize both offensive and defensive cybersecurity strategies and reshape the threat landscape.

I. Quantum Computing: A Paradigm Shift

Quantum computing leverages the principles of quantum mechanics to perform calculations in ways that classical computers cannot. Key concepts include:

- **Qubits:** Unlike classical bits, which can be either 0 or 1, qubits can exist in a superposition of both states simultaneously, allowing quantum computers to perform massive parallel computations.
- **Entanglement:** Entanglement is a quantum phenomenon where two or more qubits become linked, even when separated by vast distances. This enables quantum computers to perform certain calculations exponentially faster than classical computers.

- **Quantum Algorithms:** Quantum algorithms are designed to leverage the unique capabilities of quantum computers to solve specific problems, such as factoring large numbers or searching unsorted databases, with unprecedented efficiency.

II. Quantum Computing's Impact on Cryptography

Quantum computing poses a significant challenge to current cryptographic systems:

- **Breaking Existing Cryptography:**
    - o **Shor's Algorithm:** This quantum algorithm can efficiently factor large numbers and solve discrete logarithm problems, rendering widely used public-key cryptography algorithms like RSA and ECC vulnerable.
    - o **Grover's Algorithm:** This quantum algorithm can speed up the search for collisions in hash functions, potentially weakening their security.
    - o **Impact on Symmetric Cryptography:** While Grover's algorithm could also affect symmetric encryption, increasing the key length (e.g., using AES-256) is generally considered sufficient to mitigate this threat.
- **The Rise of Post-Quantum Cryptography (PQC):**

- o **Lattice-based Cryptography:** Relies on the difficulty of solving mathematical problems involving lattices.
- o **Code-based Cryptography:** Uses error-correcting codes to create encryption schemes.
- o **Hash-based Cryptography:** Uses hash functions in new ways to create secure digital signatures.
- o **Multivariate Polynomial Cryptography:** Relies on the difficulty of solving systems of multivariate polynomial equations.
- o **Isogeny-based Cryptography:** Uses the mathematics of elliptic curves in a way that is resistant to known quantum attacks.

III. Quantum-Enhanced Cybersecurity

Quantum computing also offers opportunities to enhance cybersecurity:

- • **Quantum Key Distribution (QKD):** QKD uses the principles of quantum mechanics to securely distribute encryption keys, making it theoretically impossible for eavesdroppers to intercept them.
- • **Quantum Random Number Generators (QRNGs):** QRNGs generate truly random numbers based on quantum phenomena, which are crucial for cryptographic

applications and enhance the security of random number generation.

- **Quantum-Resistant Algorithms:** Researchers are actively developing new cryptographic algorithms that are believed to be resistant to attacks from both classical and quantum computers. These algorithms will form the foundation of secure communication and data protection in the post-quantum era.

IV. Quantum Computing and Offensive Cybersecurity

Quantum computing can also be leveraged by attackers to enhance their capabilities:

- **Accelerated Brute-Force Attacks:** Quantum computers could potentially speed up brute-force attacks, making it easier to crack passwords and encryption keys.
- **Enhanced Cryptanalysis:** Quantum algorithms could be used to develop new cryptanalysis techniques that break existing cryptographic systems more efficiently.
- **Quantum AI:** Quantum computing could accelerate the development of AI, potentially leading to more sophisticated AI-powered attacks, such as advanced malware and adaptive social engineering campaigns.

V. Preparing for the Quantum Cybersecurity Landscape

The transition to a post-quantum world requires proactive steps to ensure the continued security of digital infrastructure:

- **Standardization:** Adopt and implement standardized PQC algorithms as they become available.
- **Algorithm Agility:** Design systems that can easily switch to new cryptographic algorithms in the future to adapt to the evolving threat landscape.
- **Hybrid Approaches:** Combine classical and post-quantum cryptography to provide security during the transition period and ensure a smooth migration to quantum-resistant systems.
- **Key Management:** Develop robust key management systems for PQC algorithms to ensure secure storage, distribution, and rotation of cryptographic keys.
- **Awareness and Education:** Raise awareness about the quantum threat and educate stakeholders about PQC, emphasizing the importance of preparedness and proactive measures.

VI. Real-World Examples and Initiatives

- **NIST Post-Quantum Cryptography Standardization:** NIST is actively evaluating and standardizing PQC algorithms to prepare for the post-quantum era, fostering the development and adoption of quantum-resistant solutions.

- **Quantum Key Distribution (QKD) Networks:** Several countries are investing in the development of QKD networks to secure critical infrastructure and government communication, demonstrating the practical application of quantum technologies for enhanced security.

- **Industry Initiatives:** Various industry consortia and organizations are working to develop and promote quantum-resistant technologies and best practices, fostering collaboration and knowledge sharing to address the challenges of the quantum era.

VII. The Future of Quantum Cybersecurity

The future of cybersecurity in the age of quantum computing is dynamic and multifaceted. Key trends and considerations include:

- **Quantum-Resistant Infrastructure:** The development and deployment of quantum-resistant infrastructure and systems will be crucial to ensure the long-term security of digital communications and data protection.

- **Quantum-Enhanced Security Solutions:** Quantum technologies like QKD and QRNGs will be integrated into security solutions to provide enhanced protection against both classical and quantum attacks.

- **Ethical Considerations:** The ethical implications of quantum computing in cybersecurity, particularly regarding privacy and surveillance, will need careful consideration and responsible development.

- **International Collaboration:** International collaboration and cooperation will be essential to address the global challenges of quantum cybersecurity and ensure a secure and stable digital future for all.

Quantum computing is poised to revolutionize cybersecurity, presenting both challenges and opportunities. By understanding the implications of quantum computing, proactively adopting quantum-resistant technologies, and fostering a culture of innovation and collaboration, we can navigate the complexities of this new era and build a secure and resilient digital future in the age of quantum computing.

CHAPTER 34: CYBERSECURITY FOR THE HUMAN-MACHINE PARTNERSHIP

As technology advances, the lines between human and machine capabilities are blurring. The future of cybersecurity will increasingly rely on a collaborative partnership between humans and machines, leveraging the unique strengths of each to create a more secure and resilient digital world. This chapter explores the evolving landscape of human-machine teaming in cybersecurity, examining the benefits, challenges, and ethical considerations of this synergistic approach.

I. The Synergy of Human and Machine Intelligence

Humans and machines possess complementary strengths that, when combined, can create a powerful force for cybersecurity:

- **Human Strengths:**
    - **Creativity and Intuition:** Humans excel at creative problem-solving, pattern recognition, and adapting to unforeseen situations.
    - **Critical Thinking and Contextual Awareness:** Humans can analyze complex scenarios, understand context, and make nuanced judgments.

- **Ethical Reasoning and Empathy:** Humans can consider ethical implications, exercise judgment, and empathize with the human impact of security decisions.

- **Machine Strengths:**
  - **Speed and Scalability:** Machines can process vast amounts of data and perform repetitive tasks with speed and accuracy.
  - **Pattern Recognition and Anomaly Detection:** Machines can identify patterns and anomalies in data that might be missed by humans.
  - **Automation and Efficiency:** Machines can automate tasks, freeing up human analysts to focus on higher-level tasks.

II. Human-Machine Teaming in Cybersecurity

The collaboration between humans and machines is transforming various cybersecurity domains:

- **Threat Detection and Response:**
  - **AI-Powered Threat Hunting:** Machines can analyze vast datasets to identify potential threats, while human analysts can investigate and validate those findings.

- o **Automated Incident Response:** Machines can automate initial incident response tasks, such as isolating infected systems, while human analysts can focus on complex decision-making and recovery efforts.

- **Vulnerability Management:**
  - o **AI-Assisted Vulnerability Discovery:** Machines can identify potential vulnerabilities in code, while human analysts can assess the severity and exploitability of those vulnerabilities.
  - o **Automated Patching and Remediation:** Machines can automate the patching process, while human analysts can oversee and validate the results.

- **Security Operations:**
  - o **AI-Powered Security Monitoring:** Machines can monitor network traffic, system logs, and user behavior for suspicious activity, while human analysts can investigate and respond to potential threats.
  - o **Security Automation and Orchestration:** Machines can automate security tasks and orchestrate workflows, improving efficiency and reducing human error.

- **Threat Intelligence:**

- o **AI-Driven Threat Intelligence Gathering:** Machines can collect and analyze threat intelligence from various sources, while human analysts can interpret and contextualize that information.
- o **Threat Prediction and Modeling:** Machines can use historical data and machine learning to predict future threats, while human analysts can assess the credibility and potential impact of those predictions.

III. Challenges and Considerations

While human-machine teaming offers significant benefits, it also presents challenges and considerations:

- **Trust and Explainability:** Building trust in AI systems and ensuring their decisions are explainable and transparent is crucial for effective collaboration.
- **Human-Machine Interface:** Designing intuitive and effective interfaces for human-machine interaction is essential for seamless collaboration.
- **Skills and Training:** Cybersecurity professionals need to develop new skills and adapt to working alongside AI systems.
- **Bias and Fairness:** Addressing potential biases in AI models and ensuring fairness in security decisions is critical.

- **Ethical Considerations:** The ethical implications of human-machine teaming, particularly regarding autonomy and decision-making, require careful consideration.

IV. Real-World Examples

- **AI-Powered Security Operations Centers (SOCs):** Many organizations are using AI to enhance their SOCs, enabling faster threat detection and response.
- **Autonomous Malware Analysis:** AI is being used to automate the analysis of malware samples, freeing up human analysts for more complex tasks.
- **Human-in-the-Loop Threat Hunting:** Security teams are using AI to assist in threat hunting, combining machine intelligence with human expertise.

V. The Future of Human-Machine Partnership in Cybersecurity

The future of cybersecurity will be characterized by an increasingly close partnership between humans and machines. Key trends and considerations include:

- **Augmented Intelligence:** AI will augment human intelligence, providing insights and recommendations to enhance decision-making.

- **Adaptive Cybersecurity:** AI systems will adapt to evolving threats and changing environments, enabling more proactive and resilient security.
- **Human-Centered AI:** The design and development of AI systems will prioritize human needs and values, ensuring ethical and responsible use.
- **Continuous Learning and Adaptation:** Both humans and machines will need to continuously learn and adapt to stay ahead of the evolving threat landscape.

The human-machine partnership is transforming cybersecurity, creating a more powerful and adaptive defense against cyber threats. By leveraging the unique strengths of humans and machines, we can build a more secure and resilient digital future. As AI continues to evolve, the collaboration between humans and machines will become even more critical in navigating the complexities of the cybersecurity landscape and protecting our digital world.

CHAPTER 35: CYBERSECURITY IN THE AGE OF BIO-DIGITAL CONVERGENCE

The lines between the physical and digital worlds are blurring as technology advances. Bio-digital convergence, the integration of biological and digital systems, is creating new frontiers in healthcare, human augmentation, and brain-computer interfaces. This chapter explores the unique cybersecurity challenges and opportunities presented by this convergence, examining how to secure the interconnected systems that bridge the human body and the digital realm.

I. Understanding Bio-Digital Convergence

Bio-digital convergence encompasses a range of technologies that integrate biological and digital systems, including:

- **Biomedical Devices and Implants:** Implantable medical devices, such as pacemakers, insulin pumps, and brain-computer interfaces, connect to digital networks for monitoring, control, and data exchange.
- **Wearable Technology:** Wearable devices, such as smartwatches and fitness trackers, collect and transmit personal health data and connect to digital ecosystems.

- **Biometric Authentication:** Biometric systems, such as fingerprint scanners and facial recognition, use biological traits for authentication and access control.

- **Genetic Engineering and Synthetic Biology:** Advances in genetic engineering and synthetic biology are creating new possibilities for manipulating biological systems, raising new cybersecurity concerns.

- **Brain-Computer Interfaces (BCIs):** BCIs enable direct communication between the brain and external devices, opening up new frontiers in human augmentation and rehabilitation, but also introducing new security risks.

II. Unique Cybersecurity Challenges

Bio-digital convergence presents unique cybersecurity challenges:

- **Human-Machine Interface Security:** Securing the interface between humans and machines is crucial to prevent unauthorized access, data breaches, and manipulation of bio-digital systems.

- **Data Privacy and Security:** Protecting sensitive personal health data collected and transmitted by bio-digital devices is paramount.

- **Device Security:** Securing biomedical devices and implants from cyberattacks is critical to prevent malfunctions, data breaches, or even life-threatening situations.

- **Integrity and Authenticity:** Ensuring the integrity and authenticity of data and commands transmitted between bio-digital systems is essential for safe and reliable operation.

- **Ethical and Legal Considerations:** The ethical and legal implications of bio-digital convergence, particularly regarding privacy, autonomy, and informed consent, require careful consideration.

III. Threats and Vulnerabilities

Bio-digital systems face a range of cyber threats:

- **Unauthorized Access and Control:** Attackers could gain unauthorized access to bio-digital devices, potentially manipulating their functions, stealing data, or causing harm to the user.

- **Data Breaches and Privacy Violations:** Sensitive personal health data could be stolen or leaked in data breaches, compromising patient privacy and confidentiality.

- **Device Manipulation and Malfunction:** Attackers could manipulate the functionality of biomedical devices, potentially causing malfunctions or delivering incorrect dosages of medication.

- **Denial-of-Service Attacks:** Attackers could launch denial-of-service attacks against bio-digital systems, disrupting their operation and potentially denying critical care.
- **Impersonation and Spoofing:** Attackers could impersonate authorized users or spoof biometric authentication systems to gain access to sensitive data or systems.

IV. Securing Bio-Digital Systems

Protecting bio-digital systems requires a comprehensive and multi-layered approach:

- **Secure Device Design and Development:** Incorporate security into the design and development of bio-digital devices from the outset, considering the unique challenges of the human-machine interface.
- **Secure Communication:** Implement secure communication protocols and encryption to protect data transmitted between bio-digital devices and other systems.
- **Device Authentication and Authorization:** Implement strong authentication and authorization mechanisms to control access to devices and data.

- **Data Protection and Privacy:** Employ data encryption, access controls, and privacy-preserving techniques to protect sensitive personal health information.

- **Vulnerability Management and Patching:** Regularly assess and remediate vulnerabilities in bio-digital devices and systems.

- **Incident Response:** Develop and exercise incident response plans to effectively handle security incidents and minimize downtime.

- **Ethical and Legal Frameworks:** Establish ethical guidelines and legal frameworks to govern the development and use of bio-digital technologies, ensuring privacy, safety, and accountability.

V. Real-World Examples and Case Studies

- **Implantable Medical Device Vulnerabilities:** Researchers have demonstrated vulnerabilities in implantable medical devices, such as pacemakers and insulin pumps, highlighting the potential for cyberattacks to compromise patient safety.

- **Data Breaches in Healthcare:** Healthcare organizations have experienced data breaches that exposed sensitive patient information, emphasizing the need for strong data protection measures in bio-digital systems.

- **Biometric Authentication Vulnerabilities:** Researchers have demonstrated vulnerabilities in biometric authentication systems, such as fingerprint scanners and facial recognition, highlighting the need for robust security measures to prevent spoofing and impersonation attacks.

VI. The Future of Bio-Digital Cybersecurity

The future of bio-digital cybersecurity will be shaped by:

- **Advancements in Bio-Digital Technologies:** New bio-digital technologies, such as brain-computer interfaces and genetic engineering, will introduce new security challenges and require innovative security solutions.
- **AI and Machine Learning:** AI and machine learning will play an increasingly important role in securing bio-digital systems, enabling real-time threat detection, anomaly detection, and automated response.
- **Ethical and Legal Frameworks:** The development of robust ethical and legal frameworks will be crucial to guide the responsible development and use of bio-digital technologies.
- **Human-Machine Collaboration:** The future of bio-digital cybersecurity will rely on a close collaboration between humans and machines, leveraging the strengths of each to create a secure and trustworthy bio-digital ecosystem.

Securing bio-digital systems is a critical challenge in the age of converging technologies. By understanding the unique vulnerabilities, adopting a comprehensive security approach, and staying ahead of emerging threats, we can protect the integrity, privacy, and safety of these systems and enable the responsible development and use of bio-digital technologies for the benefit of humanity.

www.ingramcontent.com/pod-product-compliance
Lightning Source LLC
LaVergne TN
LVHW051322050326
832903LV00031B/3315